Meditation: The Mystic Path

Sean Williams

Copyright © 2010 by Sean Williams

All rights reserved by the author. No part of this publication may be reproduced, stored in a retrieval system or transmitted in any form or by any means electronic, mechanical, photocopying, recording or otherwise, without the prior written permission of the author.

ISBN: 978-0-615-35192-6

Sean Williams

A UNIVERSAL UNDERSTANDING

First of all, I'd like to say congratulations to you my friend, for you have been chosen to receive the greatest gift that can be given, the gift of knowledge. What you do with it is entirely up to you. I have written this book specifically to record my own understanding of transcendental consciousness. This physical body is a humble servant of the divine will. I am a normal person who has taken the path less traveled (*less traveled only because it has been hidden*). Being that I never completed college, you will find that my limited vocabulary has helped me keep it simple. By studying my simple understanding, maybe you will begin to form your own simple understanding. My hope is with you!

"Let there be one among you who understands", Jesus, in the Gospel of Thomas.

Okay, now let's get started...

WHAT IS MYSTICISM?

The "Wikipedia" (free online encyclopedia) has an easy to understand definition (overview) of what Mysticism is. Mysticism (from the Greek term, "mystikos", an initiate (*the "holy" person at the beginning of any religion*) of a mystery religion, i.e. Jesus, Buddha, Mohamed, Moses, etc.), is the pursuit of communion with, to identify with, or a conscious awareness of, an ultimate reality, divinity (*the divine will*), spiritual truth, or God through direct experience, intuition, or insight (*meditation*). **Mysticism usually centers on a practice or practices intended to nurture that experience or awareness.**

Mysticism may be dualistic, maintaining a distinction between the self and the divine, or may be nondualistic. Differing religious traditions have described this fundamental mystical experience in different ways:

- Complete detachment from the "world" (Kaivalya in Yoga; Samadhi in Hinduism, Jhana in Buddhism)

- Liberation from the cycles of Karma (Moksha in Jainism, Nirvana in Hinduism and Buddhism)

- Deep intrinsic connection to the world (Satori in Mahayana Buddhism, Te in Taoism)
- Union with God (Henosis in Neo-Platonism and Theosis in Christianity)
- Innate Knowledge (Irfan and fitra in Islam)

"Enlightenment" or "Illumination", are generic English terms for the phenomenon, derived from the Latin "illuminatio" (applied to Christian prayer in the 15th century) and adopted in English translations of Buddhist texts, but loosely to describe the state of mystical attainment regardless of faith.

Mystic traditions generally form sub-currents within larger religious traditions-such as Kabbalah within Judaism, Sufism within Islam, Vedanta within Hinduism, and Christian mysticism within Christianity- but are often treated skeptically and held separate, due to their emphasis on personal experience over doctrine. Mysticism is sometimes taken by skeptics or mainstream adherents as mere obfuscation, though mystics suggest they are offering clarity of a different kind.

Being that all religions refer to "teachings" set forth into "the world" by these "Mystics" (*those with a complete "connection" to the divine*) then one must understand that Mysticism predates all "worldly" religions. The overall goal of "worldly" religions, is supposedly to help us reunite as individuals with the "divine" (*God, a.k.a. "go to heaven"*), which is fundamental Mysticism. Therefore, "Mysticism" is found at the beginning, core, and end of all religions. Thus, more attention needs to be paid to the "practices" of the ancient "Mystics", which have been hidden from "the world", by the leaders of "organized" religion.

The "practices" the ancient mystics used to become in union with the "divine will", generally center around the use of visionary entheogenic plants and potions, known as "Mystic Communion", and deep introspective meditation (*known as looking within, where Jesus say's God and the kingdom are found*). "Practices" designed to evolve ones consciousness beyond the physical.

WHAT IS "MYSTIC COMMUNION"?

Understand that before the creation of "the Bible", there was no such thing as a "forbidden" fruit. "Mystic Communion" is simply consumption of the true "Fruit of Knowledge", which "awakens" your spiritual self (*the kundalini*) so that you can communicate with and receive guidance from the non-physical. "Organized Religion" has become quite profitable by preventing us from individually communicating with the non-physical (*the divine, God*) without them or their collection plates, therefore they have a real reason to prevent the true identity and purpose of the "fruit of knowledge" from coming out. If we all figure out that the true temple is within, then we won't go back to "church" and they will lose their "contributions" with which they have become quite comfortable.

"Mystic Communion" is what is described as "Manna", in the Bible. Although again they said "Manna" ceased to exist after Moses' death. Again they lied! "Manna", "Fruit of knowledge", "Forbidden fruit", these are all one in the same thing, it is psilocybin mushrooms. Jesus referred to them as the "Keys of Knowledge". The Native Americans, and Native Mexicans, also used peyote, but mainly it's psilocybin mushrooms that were used in their rituals. The Mayan's called psilocybin mushrooms, "Teonanactl" (*flesh of the gods*), and used them In rituals as high as in the coronation of rulers. The Aztecs used them ritualistically as well. Psilocybin mushrooms are an "Entheogen". Mystic Communion can be any of the entheogens, but for logic reasons, one must understand the occurrence rate and likely hood that you'd come across them in the wild. Understanding that they occur naturally in the dung of livestock, psilocybin mushrooms logically would appear much more frequently near populated areas if the conditions are right than most of the others. This is a coincidental explanation of why, most of the religious figures, throughout history, are known as "shepherds".

Psilocybin Mushrooms are powerful entheogens and are relatively safe on a toxicity level. They are quite easy to cultivate on sterilized "cakes", when which prepared correctly, they are less toxic than aspirin (rated by the National Institute for Occupational Safety and Health, a branch of the Center of Disease Control). There has never been an overdose fatality from psilocybin mushrooms. Tea can be made from psilocybin mushrooms for an intoxicating brew. There is no doubt in my mind that psilocybin mushrooms were served at "the Last Supper" of Christ and the Apostles. The importance of these amazing "fruit" has been suppressed by society due to the fear that once people begin to realize the truth, and see the organized religious churches differently, people will wake up and stop consuming all the unnecessary stuff. Society as we know it could collapse. Therefore the truth has been hidden...

Jesus, in "The Gospel of Thomas" #66

"Jesus said, "Show me the stone that the builders rejected: that is the keystone."

"Gospel of Thomas" #39 Jesus said, "The Pharisees and the scholars have taken the keys of knowledge and have hidden them. They have not entered nor have they allowed those who want to enter to do so.

WHAT IS AN "AWAKENING"?

There are many forms of the same understanding when it comes to the "awakening". There is the Kundalini awakening, the awakening of the spiritual consciousness in you, forming the transcendental consciousness (spirit body). At its basic level "an awakening", is simply the first significant step of the evolution of one's spiritual consciousness. When one has an intense psychedelic experience, many times they feel as though they've "woken up" mentally and are no longer at the will of their physical desires. They often then begin the path of purification of the mind and sometimes even asceticism dedicated to denying themselves worldly pleasures with the purpose of focusing on the goal of spiritual growth rather than physical indulgence which impedes spiritual focus. To outside friends, family, and acquaintances, it simply appears as a shift in the overall priorities of the "awakened" individual. The changes can be alarming to those who don't understand.

WHAT IS MEDITATION?

From the Wikipedia, "Meditation is a mental discipline by which one attempts to get beyond the reflexive, "thinking" (*physical*) mind into a deeper state of relaxation or awareness. Meditation often involves turning attention to a single point of reference. It is a component of many religions and has been practiced since antiquity. It is also practiced outside of religious traditions. Different meditative disciplines encompasses a wide range of spiritual or psychophysical practices that may emphasize different goals—from achievement of a higher state of consciousness, to greater focus, creativity or self-awareness, or simply a more relaxed and peaceful frame of mind.

The word *meditation* comes from the Indo-European root *med-*, meaning "to measure". It entered English as *meditation* through the Latin meditation, which originally indicated any type of physical or intellectual exercise, then later evolved into the more specific meaning "contemplation"."

The "deepest" forms of meditation include activation of "Kundalini" flowing through "Nadi" and "the gates" (a.k.a. chakras) from "Root, to Crown and beyond". There is no doubt that psychedelic mushrooms can aide in the process of "Kundalini awakening", other meditational methods can also aid in the focusing of attention and conscious release (*letting go*) of the physical mind which is required to become fully awakened, but psychedelic mushrooms are definitely a key which allows anyone, anywhere, a way to find their way to full spiritual consciousness if they were inclined to seek it.

Meditation has become known to some as "the path to God", and the way to attain "immortality". The key to attaining immortality is to realize the truth, you are not physical. Detach from the physical world and attain full spiritual consciousness, by simply letting go of the physical consciousness.

MYSTICS FROM THE PAST HAVE LEFT CLUES FOR US TO FOLLOW:

The Cathars understood the truth, but were wiped out by the Catholics during the inquisition. During this time of the birth and spread of organized religion, a great many of the Great Mystics left clues for others to follow on their journeys back to spiritual consciousness, but they were lost to bonfires and other destruction during the Inquisition. Yet a few remain. The Gospel of Thomas is one of these very documents. The true translation of the Dead Sea Scrolls, in the original edition of "The Sacred Mushroom and The Cross", is another. The Wikipedia version of the five levels of psychedelic experience is another. Once you understand truth, you realize your duty to try and tell "the world", as the mystics have done since the beginning of "time".

HOW TO CULTIVATE PSILOCYBIN MUSHROOMS, SO YOU TOO CAN PARTAKE IN "MYSTIC COMMUNION".

Ok first off, I must say thanks to the innovators who have come before me, Psylocybe Fanaticus, Erowid and "The Magic Mushroom Growers Guide", without their vast experimentation, and understandings I might have never "woken up" to the "True Reality" of things, grim as it may be. A very thorough step-by-step (*although a bit scientifically expansive and therefore confusing and frustrating, due to different techniques*) process can be found by looking up "The magic mushroom growers guide" on the internet. I'm the type of person who likes to simplify things so I'm just going to get to the point and detail the best way I've found to grow them (*for educational, and spiritual purposes only, of course*).

IT IS VERY IMPORTANT THAT YOU KNOW, CULTIVATION OF THESE "MIND EXPANDING" FRUITS HAS BEEN DEEMED ILLEGAL BY THE FEDERAL GOVERNMENT (the man), AND PUNISHMENT CAN BE INCURRED FROM ANYONE BEING CAUGHT GROWING THESE "SHROOMS" FOR PURPOSES OF DISTRIBUTION.

The "psychedelic experience" is undoubtedly responsible for the entire "flower child", "hippie", 60's, 70's and "Woodstock" eras. Magic Mushrooms were at one time, sold legally in shops in Amsterdam all year long because they believed in individual discretion and freedom.

Another thing I must say is that the real "Magic" in these mushrooms, is their ability to separate your spiritual and physical selves, so that you can too have your own "religious experience". I cannot guarantee the safety of "wild" "magic" mushrooms, due to too many unknown variables (*unknown toxins*) in different contaminates (*other types of fungus*) that have access to the same growing media that the "shrooms" themselves come from. But undoubtedly, humans since the beginning of time have consumed nature's "Fruit of Knowledge" to find their spiritual selves. If you intend to look for natural "Shrooms", then consume them at your own risk. The hallucinogenic compound "psilocybin" occurs in over a hundred of different types of mushrooms and the only real "give away" to its presence in a natural "shroom" is, when you cut into the shroom, it should turn blue, which is a reaction to the psilocybin and oxygen.

The safest way that you too can have your own mystic "religious experience", is by growing your own "Shrooms" on completely sterilized growth "cakes". When you manage to grow some of these "pure" (*contaminate free*) "shrooms", they are no more toxic than a cigarette, aspirin, or caffeine, and they definitely aren't poisonous. These "pure" mushrooms, have the ability to help you on your road to enlightenment by helping you tap into the universal consciousness and the cash of information that is stored there. Buddhists call it gaining experience from past lives, Christians and Catholics call it invoking the "Holy Spirit", Indians and mystics call it a spirit journey. I call it an understanding of a truth that cannot be taught by another physical person.

The truth of the matter is that many people may not be able to go to a "level 5" "complete" experience. For a "physically bound" person it is a frightening experience. The purely physical mind and "ego" is not capable or comfortable accepting spiritual knowledge, and due to the separation anxiety that happens, when you become spiritually separate, your physical self "feels" as if it's dying, but it isn't actually "you", it is only your "ego" and your "physical nature" that is dying. But due to that "feeling" most people are simply too afraid to have a "full" experience.

These "Forbidden Fruit" have been used by Mystics, Indians, and Spiritualists, to gain perspective of themselves and "the world", since before organized religion. True "mystics", "fast" for several days (*don't eat anything, or very little and selectively for five days*), before consuming their "shrooms", in order to purify their bodies and strengthen their minds, in order to have a more complete, spiritual experience. (*They weaken their physical self, to empower their spiritual self.*)

Jesus in "The Gospel of Thomas": #69 Congratulations to those who go hungry, so the stomach of the one in want may be filled."

WHAT YOU WILL NEED IN ORDER TO GROW "PURE" SHROOMS (FOR EDUCATIONAL PURPOSES):

The "Shrooms" grow on sterilized vermiculite and brown rice flour "cubes".

So you will, at the least, need some medium grain vermiculite and some healthfood store "organic" quality brown rice flour. You will also need some distilled water (*non-tap water is best*) and some ½ pint mason jars. Beginners, you must use ½ pint jars, 1 pint jars take too long to become ready and contamination usually results, ending in failure.

To get started, go to the local "Mart" store and buy some ½ pint mason jars, a Styrofoam cooler, some silicone, some cloth tape, some gallon zip lock bags, a box of 5 gallon extra large zip lock bags two foil deep baking pans, a foil cookie sheet, an ultrasonic humidifier, a metal grate (for the cooler), another metal grate (for the dehydrator) and an 8qt pressure cooker.

Go to the hardware store and buy a 5/8 drill bit, a piece of Plexiglas, some clear vinyl tubing, some grommets, some desiccant and some brackets big enough to fit around a two-liter bottle.

Most department stores do not carry vermiculite, only perlite, which won't work. To get vermiculite you need to go find a place that sells bulk lawn care and fertilizer items. That was the hardest thing for me to find but don't get discouraged, enlightenment is definitely worth the work….

You will also need some "spore syringes". "Spores" are simply seeds of mushroom bearing fungus. These can be bought from any spore bank, there are many on the internet. Spores are completely legal to buy and ship as long as they are for studying purposes only. Simply look up the key word "spores". One of the best types for beginners are "Pesa" type, Psilocybe cubensis Amazon type, but my favorite is the "Orissa" type, for their incredibly large size capability and original growing location was in Orissa India, along the "path" that Jesus supposedly traveled during his "missing" years from the bible. (*The years between his youth and the age where his life became chronicled in the Bible, and other Gnostic, and Buddhist texts*) He undoubtedly had access to these "mind expanding" fruits, and his belief in their abilities, might have been what caused the "Roman Catholics" (*the same people who crucified him*) to deem them "forbidden".

SPIRITUAL ORIGINS OF THE ORISSA STRAIN:

A little bit more about the location in which the "Orissa" type shrooms were originally found, helps add to their spirituality. They were found growing from a large pile of elephant dung (*elephants are considered sacred in India*), along the Narmada River at the foot of the Vindhya hills.

Narmada, a Sanskrit word means "One who endows with bliss". It flows from east to west and serves as the traditional boundary between North India and South India. (*As we are in purgatory between heaven and hell*) It originates from a small tank called Narmada Kund located on the Amarkantak hill.

Religious significance of the Narmada River: The Narmada happens to be one of the most sacred of the five holy rivers of India; the other four being Ganga, Yamuna, Godavari and Kaveri. It is believed that a dip in any of these five rivers washes ones sins away. According to a legend, the river Ganga is polluted by millions of people bathing in it. To cleanse herself, Ganga acquires the form of a black cow (*an also sacred creature*) and comes to the Narmada to bathe in its holy waters.

The place where it originates is named Amarkantak. It is a pilgrim town and a "nagar panchayat" in Anuppur District in the state of Madhya Pradesh, India. Also called "Teerthraj" (the king of pilgrimages), Amarkantak region is a unique natural heritage area and is the meeting point of the Vindhyas and the Satpuras, with the Maikal Hills being the fulcrum. This is the place from where the Narmada River, the Sone River and Johila River emerge.

As the source of the Narmada, which is more than 150 million years older than the Ganga and is considered by many hindus to be the most sacred of all the rivers of India, Amarkantak itself is sacred to the Hindus and is deemed to be a door-way to 'nirwana'. In the Amarkantak hills dwell some of the most primitive of the Madhya Pradesh tribals, the Hill Korwas and Pandavas. Even today, the Pandavas run away if they see any strangers approaching their village.

Religious importance of Amarkantak: Amarkantak situated on the western edge of ancient Kingdom of Kalinga is a place of worship for all the three worlds. Gods and Gandharvas (Celestial beings), Asuras (demons), Saints and Sages have all achieved great spiritual powers here. It is believed that whoever dies at Amarkantak is assured of a place in heaven.

Amarkantak is a Sanskrit word, the literal meaning of which is immortal (amar) obstruction (kantak). The place was the abode of Gods but was disturbed by the hindrances of Rudraganas and hence called Amarkantak.

OK NOW, FOR THE EASIEST WAY TO GROW SPIRITUAL MEDICINE:

You need to combine measured amounts of the brown rice flour and vermiculite. I like to cook my flour and vermiculite separately in the oven before mixing to add to the sterility of the project. I put the bulk measurement of each ingredient into a deep foil pan and heat them both to 300 degrees in the oven for 30 minutes. I also add an extra quart of vermiculite to the pan so I will have enough for my dry layer. A barrier layer against contaminates.

The mix consists of 2/3 cup of vermiculite and ¼ cup brown rice flour for each ½ pint jar you intend to use. The typical 10cc spore syringe will prepare ten jars, so I like to prepare my mix in bulk. I mix 1qt and 2 2/3 cups of Vermiculite with 2 ½ cups of brown rice flour in a large mixing bowl which equals ten half pint jars. I mix the two in the bowl, with a butter knife, until I cannot see any separation of the different ingredients. That is the easy part. You need to boil the distilled water for about ten minutes to kill off any bacteria in the water. Once you begin to pour in the water, it will become much more difficult to mix, but you cannot stop.

The proper amount of water for each jar is ¼ cup of water for each ½ pint jar, but since I'm mixing in bulk, I use 2 ½ cups of boiled water for the entire amount in the bowl. Pour the water in a little at a time mixing thoroughly, difficult as it is (*it almost feels like mixing concrete*), until the mixture's consistency looks like oatmeal cookie dough with no obvious dry spots. (*yes, your arm will get tired!*)

After you are done mixing, fill each jar with the mixture up to the bottom threads on the jar. Don't pack it tight, small gaps and holes in the mix are good! Wipe the tops of the jars from the bottom of the threads up, completely clean (*spotless!*) and then fill up (*top off*) the rest of the jar to the top with dry vermiculite. Make four holes in each lid before you put the lids on the jar. You make the holes for two things, first you need to be able to inject spores into the jar without opening the lid, and second, the jars will explode when you heat them up, if you don't.

After you are done filling, cleaning, topping off, and you've put your lid with holes in it tightly onto the jar, you need to cover the lids with tin foil so that when you boil the jars, water won't get into the holes and turn your hard work into mud.

Ok, the next step after you've prepared your jars is simple. The cheap way is to get a large pot and put as many of the jars in as you can. It's best to keep them off of the bottom somehow because the high heat will cause the jars to crack. I use a small metal grate, or a couple of dish cloths. The best and fastest way is to use a pressure cooker. The jars need to boil in a regular pot for an hour. You don't want the jars floating around. Only put enough water into the pot so that it comes up to a little past half way up the jars. With a regular pot, you need to constantly monitor the water level to make sure you don't boil away all of your water. It's cheaper, but it's a lot more time consuming and the margin for error and lost jars is greater. With a pressure cooker the time is cut down to about 25-30 minutes and your sterilization percentage is much better. Pressure cookers range from 35$ to 200$+, but the 35-45$ versions work great.

After you have finished cooking your jars, take them out of the pot and place them into zip lock bags and allow them to cool for at least six hours (*overnight is best*).

After the jars have cooled down to room temperature (*between 70-82 degrees*), it is time to inoculate (*put the spores in*). Shake your spore syringe well to make sure the spores are well dispersed into the liquid. You can insert the needles of your spore syringes into the holes you made on the lid. Make it so that the hole in the tip of the needle is facing the glass. Timing in this case is important. Most spore banks use dehydrated spores in their spore syringes. Once they prepare a syringe for you and ship it to you, it's only good for at most two weeks. It's best to have your jars prepared and ready to inoculate with spores on the day they arrive.

Now squirt just a little bit of the liquid into each hole in the lid. You only need 1 total cc. (*a little extra won't hurt*) for each jar, so the liquid should form a spot the size of a dime on the inside wall of the glass.

After you have squirted 1cc. into your jar put a piece of cloth tape (*breathable*) over each hole to prevent small bugs from getting in and messing it up. The cloth tape also helps protect against bad mold spores from getting in and contaminating your jar.

The next part is easy. Put them in a warm (*80-82 degrees is perfect! Not over 85 or below 75*), dark place and wait. (*Don't get impatient, just let them do their thing*) After a week you should begin to see small patches of white fuzz. That white fuzz is good, that's what you've worked so hard for. After two weeks you should be able to see large areas of the jar covered with the white fuzz. And after three weeks most of the jar should be white. Sometimes it takes longer but if your mix is right it should take no longer than 1 ½ months to become fully ready to "fruit". (*If they aren't ready by then, something went wrong! Probable contamination.*)

After the entire surface is covered by white fuzz, inspect it very carefully to make sure there are no other colors. If there are other colors, throw it away! Other colors green, brown, pink, or anything except white, are signs of contamination and your media is bad. Don't risk it, just throw it away!

If the contents of your jar are completely white, then you are ready to birth your little beauties. But before you go popping the top on the jar, make sure you have a terrarium ready to provide your little babies a nice humid place to live.

This place is called a Terrarium. It is inexpensive to build, all you need is a styrofoam cooler with a tight fitting lid, usually 5-8$ at k-mart, and a clear piece of Plexiglas, 5-10$ at any hardware store. A perfect temperature and humidity balance can be achieved by using an ultrasonic humidifier to force cool, humid air into the cooler. It frees up a lot of the work and keeps the environment in the cooler perfect for the growth and fruiting stage. Ultrasonic humidifiers usually cost about 50$ but are well worth it.

Cut a hole in the lid of the cooler and silicone a piece of Plexiglas over it. Put a wire screen into the bottom of the cooler to keep your little white cubes off of the bottom. Make a small hole in the bottom of the cooler to let water and co2 (*shrooms breath oxygen like us!*) out.

Ultra sonic humidifiers pump out too much humidity even at the lowest setting, so you need to build a drying chamber for the humid air. Don't worry, it's easy, three 2-liter bottles, some clear plastic tubing and some grommets and you have everything you need.

Face the top of the bottle downwards with the lid down, and drill a hole in the upper side, fit one of the grommets into the hole, then drill another hole into the opposite side farther down the side, and put a grommet in that hole. Follow the same process for the two other bottles and that part is done. I like to find a way to attach my bottles to a board. This can be done cheaply with tape, or you can get clamps at the hardware store.

Space the three bottles a couple of inches apart with the grommets all facing the same way, (*high, low, high, low, high, low*) and then cut pieces of tubing long enough to reach from one bottle to the next with a little extra length just for good measure. Cut the ends of the tubes at an angle so that a drop of water doesn't form and clog the end of the tube. It's also important that you don't have any low spots in your tubing, or they will plug up. Plug the regular opening that lets the humidity out of the humidifier and drill a hole into the center of the cap big enough to tightly fit the tubing into the top of the lid. Run a length of tubing from the humidifier into the first 2 liter bottle. Drill a hole into the side of the Styrofoam cooler towards the top edge. Run another length of tubing from the third bottle into the cooler and there you are.

I like to get a thermometer with a humidity gauge in it, to place inside the cooler so that I can tell at a glance, through the Plexiglas how the environment is doing without disturbing anything.

Once your Terrarium is up and running, you can go ahead and place your completely white little babies inside of the terrarium onto the grate. It is best if you barely handle them because everywhere you touch them will not "fruit". I gently tap the jar onto its lid before opening the lid completely from the jar and then empty the contents into the lid. It should stay together (*holding its shape*) and slide out like a white moldy biscuit. Gently hold it in place as you flip it over and set it carefully right side up onto the grate. Remove the lid and let it settle into place. Put the lid with the plexi glass back onto the cooler and bask in the glory of your accomplishment.

The white cubes need to be kept at mid to low 70's for a week or so at 90% humidity in order to start growing little shrooms. They need a little light, an arctic white or similar fluorescent bulb with a high blue content does well. I use a small individual light unit with my setup dedicated specifically for my "babies". I give my setup 12 hours of light a day, but they will grow with as little as 1-2 hours. I just turn on my light before I head out to work and turn it off before I go to bed.

After initiating these little shrooms, they grow to full size a little better at a higher temp, around 80 degrees. Seven to ten days after appearing, the shrooms will be ready to pluck.

After the shrooms grow to a larger size and begin to form the brown ball on the end, then the ball will turn into a cap. As the cap begins to tear away from the stalk it is time to pluck that shroom off of your cake. It is easiest to pluck the shrooms with a twist and pull method.

The best way to keep your shrooms edible is to dehydrate them. But you cannot use heat! The best thing to do is to get a cheap foil baking pan and put some desiccant into it. You can get desiccant at any hardware store by the name of "dampness remover", humidity remover, or something like that. It is usually in the paint section. Position a wire mesh over the foil baking pan and hold it in place with tape. Be careful to not allow the desiccant to touch the wire screen or your shrooms. Put the assembly inside of an extra large airtight locking bag, the 5 gallon type work well. After a couple of days they should be dry enough to save until you have enough for a complete dose.

The typical amount of beginner "shroom" dosage ranges from 1.5 grams of dried shrooms for a mild experience, to 3.5 grams for an intense experience. My suggestion is to start with a small dose, until you get the hang of it, the feelings and thoughts that you will experience can be a little overwhelming if you don't know what to expect. You should under no circumstances eat more than 3.5 grams of dried shrooms at once if you are a beginner. Even experienced users have trouble maintaining their composure at levels above 3.5 grams. If what you are experiencing simply gets to be too much for you, then take a large dose 500-1000 milligrams of vitamin C, and a small meal and that should neutralize the effect. But remember, once the feeling is gone, it's gone, and eating more will not bring it back.

Do not eat shrooms more than once a month, not only does your body build up a tolerance to psilocybin, but you need to try and do something with the knowledge that you gained before trying to gain more.

The most important thing is to remember: YOU ARE NOT DYING! Sometimes "ego" death happens, but that is not you! It is just your negative ego-consciousness trying to maintain control! If you feel momentarily like you are going to disappear because you feel like you are leaving reality somehow, just try to calm your mind and pay attention to what you are seeing. What you are probably experiencing is a level 3-4 "trip". A trip of which allows you to experience a different "reality" (*the spiritual reality*). Mystics and Native Americans used to go to that alternate reality all the time to receive help from their spiritual guides using peyote cactus or shrooms. But the truth is, you will not go, if you don't want to, it's entirely up to you.

Definitely, under no circumstances, should you go to the hospital. They will feed you some charcoal crap and cause you to have violent stomach cramps as they try to get you to throw up, which will do nothing for you. You will still be messed up and then also feel like crap with your stomach hurting. It will only cause them, to force you to talk to some psychiatrist who thinks they have the right to analyze you, when in actuality they need to pay more attention to themselves.

But ultimately you just need to let the psilocybin run its course. The hospital can do nothing for you. I started to freak out one time on some LSD and a good friend of mine said to me: "Don't worry bro, everything's ok, just ride it out" that seemed to make me feel better.

As far as the levels of psychedelic experience go, I feel like they are deeper levels of your own consciousness that you are experiencing, or simply tests to be passed or failed. Failing these tests is common (*and scary*) for most and like any test, with practice, confidence is achieved and even the scariest barriers can be overcome.

Level 1-2 are attainable by most people and the good feelings are achieved by feeding your spiritual self.

Level 3 begins to become more intense, and your physical self begins to lose power as your spiritual self becomes more powerful. You begin to sense both of your "selfs" inside of your body.

Level 4 Your physical self becomes weaker still, and begins to fall unconscious, when this happens, thoughts of death are common due to the physical self not wanting to relinquish control of the body. Your (*negative*) physical self uses that fear trigger to get you to maintain your physical consciousness, and therefore tries to prevent your spiritual self from taking over control of your body. If you have the presence of mind, it is possible to overcome that fear and take the final step to enlightenment.

Level5 You have successfully let go of your physical self. You experience a full connection of your consciousness to the universal consciousness (*most call it "God"*). What you perceive as physical reality, is gone, but you don't care. You don't want it anyway. In the eternal moment, you realize, to be physical, is to suffer, at the will of the body's insatiable desires, the pre-programmed, food, water, procreate (*make more!*) commands. Then you realize the brainwashing nature of society, and the unnecessary desires society impresses into us, money, car, house, work, sex, food. You understand the temporal nature of physical happiness, life, the inevitable sadness/desire that comes from temporal physical satisfaction. You begin to understand that you don't necessarily want to go back. Just remaining "alive" in the "physical world" is work in itself. Taking care of your vessel (*body*) so that you can navigate the physical "world" in order to help others find truth, all the while you know your body is consuming your "life" (*energy*) is a lot to bear. You understand that everyone has a choice to make and you want to help prepare them for making the right choice. That choice is to be spiritually conscious, or physically conscious. You begin to feel as though you've somehow "woken up", to a great truth, and you need to share this experience with everyone. To choose to remain in the "world" with full knowledge of the truth makes you the "Christ" (*one who surrenders their life to remain in the world of the dead so that they may "save" the rest by teaching them the "truth", and helping them see what the one sees).*

If you truly get to level 5, congratulations, you're "The Christ", A "Buddha", or "Master Yoda". Most people get to level 4 and FREAK OUT! The first time I hit level 4, I freaked way out! I thought surely I was going to DIE from poisoning (*which is a common misconception*)! But I didn't. So then a year later, I grew another batch and tried it again. Again, I felt myself dying, and started to freak out, but then I remembered the same feeling last time and everything being okay. That thought calmed my mind, and instead of running around in circles, freaking out, with my heart racing, I sat down on the couch and relaxed. I felt myself losing physical consciousness. There were orange and green lights swirling all around me. Suddenly "I'm DYING!" popped into my mind. Then, "Oh-NO!" My heartbeat sped up and the lights faded. I looked around and saw I was still on the couch. I realized that even though I felt like I was dying, I never felt like I was going to go away, or lose consciousness. I realized that even "death" is an illusion of the physical mind and ego, which can be overcome with practice, proper focus, and psilocybin mushrooms.

THE UNIVERSAL CONSCIOUSNESS UNDERSTANDING

During my exploration of consciousness, many things have become much clearer to me. We are all seeds of consciousness, it is during the physical evolution of our consciousnesses, that we are given the intelligence required to choose whether or not we will continue evolving, and expanding our consciousness or not. Will we become stuck in the physical world and miss our opportunity to continue beyond the physical world, or will we let go of the physical and evolve to the next level?

To understand that your sperm's consciousness, came from your consciousness (life energy), makes you God and the universe, to your sperm. We are all God's sperm of consciousness.

On the consciousness level, I am the father of my sperm, as I am a Son of the father, my consciousness is "The Holy Spirit".

Compared to the consciousness of "God" (the universal consciousness), we are unconscious. Like a drop of water compared to the ocean. He has given us everything we need to expand and grow our own consciousnesses so that we can be strong enough to make the full shift from physical consciousness to spiritual consciousness. But he won't make us. He gives us what we need. What we do with what he has given us, is up to us. "Manna" was created for us in the world specifically for spiritual growth. "Manna" was and still is psilocybin mushrooms. He makes them grow naturally in the wilderness anywhere animals graze in a temperate climate with a morning dew. He leaves the decision to eat them up to us. That is free will.

Physical "worldly" desires directly inhibit spiritual growth. "Sin" in its simplest form is physical desire in any form. The desire to be "physical" in the first place was the "original sin" which we were all born with, and must "repent". Physical desire is poison to the spiritual consciousness. The poison causes one to lose consciousness. "Death" is simply the loss of conscious thought. Psilocybin mushrooms and other entheogens like peyote, and auyuaska, are different forms of the cure for our spiritual unconsciousness. Psilocybin mushrooms also help you overcome your own physical desires, by making you see them as they are, bars of your cell, which keep you trapped by your own choice. Foolish really...

Against the scope of eternity, our entire "physical" lives go by in a mere "moment". When we were poisoned with the physical desire and our consciousness evolved into physical, we lost spiritual consciousness. Therefore we "died" (fell unconscious) spiritually, and what we perceive as "life" is in actuality the "life flashing before our eyes" moment (of a fallen angel), in which we choose to return to spiritual consciousness and live by letting go of physical desire, or become attached to the physical world, and die. Learn to "surrender" your "physical" life to overcome "death".

If you devote your entire physical life to pursuing physical desires, you may become very wealthy and comfortable. If you never take any time to develop your spiritual consciousness, in the end the wealth and comfort will be your anchors (or nooses) which tie you to death by your own choice.

When you are confronted with "death" you cannot hesitate, you have to know how to let go of that which ends. You must commit yourself fully and face it or you will not shift your consciousness to spiritual and your hesitation will cause you to experience "death". If you devote some time during your "physical" life to using the "keys of knowledge" (psilocybin mushrooms) and learn to be comfortable with the shift of consciousness which happens as we leave the physical body, you will be better prepared and luck favors the prepared.

To the spiritual consciousness, the physical world is death. To learn how to let go of the physical world by eating psilocybin mushrooms, is to learn how to escape death.

We are all faced with overcoming death. Transcendence is learning how to become conscious beyond the physical world. This is a lesson which cannot be taught by any physical person. The physical consciousness is death. Learning how to let go of everything relating to the physical consciousness (worldly desires) is learning how to escape death. This can only be achieved by understanding the psychedelic experience. The answers are already within you, you only need to get beyond the distractions of the physical self to focus and understand them. Learn to connect your energy to the universal energy and everything will become clear...

The best gift I can give is the truth. Physical life is simply spiritual death. To "save" someone you must help them understand this truth. To overcome "death" one must surrender the desire to "live" physically. One must choose to surrender what they perceive as their "life" on their own, this is free will. True "death" can be avoided by simply letting go. Psychedelics have the ability to show us this very truth.

People have "bad trips" when they suddenly realize this truth and realize during physical life we are actually spiritually dying and then panic is experienced. Realize that you are already dead, and you cannot die any more than being physically conscious. Avoid death by using psychedelics to regain spiritual consciousness temporarily so that you can realize the truth before your chance passes by and you do not become trapped by ignorance. Escape death by escaping the physical world. This is a learned ability taught by the psychedelic experience.

Simply, you are eternal. You are just unconscious. What most perceive as "life" is in actuality unconsciousness (death). By learning to "let go" of physical consciousness (surrender), one learns how to wake up eternally by letting go of unconsciousness. This is the knowledge given by the fruit of knowledge.

The awakened kundalini. During our physical lives, we are meant to awaken this dormant spiritual consciousness within each of us. This is a process, which over time can overwrite the pre-programmed physical desires, such as, eat, sleep, fear, pain, make more (sex), find comfort. Those with a dormant kundalini, which is something we are each "born" into the physical world with, are easy to control or influence. Only by working to awaken this force within us all through use of psychedelic mushrooms and other entheogens, and specific yogic, meditational, mind focusing practices can we gain liberation from physical desire. To have physical desire is to suffer. To allow the kundalini to unfold within your vessel and push the physical desire out of your vessel (body) is to be removed from suffering. All we have to do is learn how to let it go.

If during your awakening process, you choose to hold onto your physical desire, you will have a hard time (bad trip). Surrender to it, don't fight it. Ride it out…

Our bodies come pre-programmed but that is not us. We are the dormant kundalini which powers the body. During our physical lives we are given an opportunity to awaken this eternal spirit within us, or seed of God's consciousness. As long as we allow our kundalini to remain dormant, we are trapped thinking with the physical mind, with the kundalini acting as a mere battery and therefore we are easier to predict and control. This is why this path is "forbidden" by those who have been made comfortable by you working for them to buy their products, spend their money, pay their taxes, and donate to their churches. Once you awaken your kundalini, you will see them for who they truly are, and they don't want that! Once you begin the path of feeding and nurturing this dormant spirit, within and focus your energy on its growth and awakening, you will have found the temple and kingdom within, and understand what it is to be "saved". "The Christ" is someone with a fully awakened kundalini. They don't want any more like him, to prove them as frauds, and ignorant fools. Which is why his true path to ascension has been concealed and his true message has been corrupted.

We exist in a "world" which has been quarantined due to the existence of evil and selfishness. Many faiths refer to this evil as "the devil", or "the serpent seed", or "the defiant spirit". Ultimately it is simply the "ego", which exists in each and every one of us. Only once we have destroyed our egos, and purified (let go of physical desire) our spirits will we then be removed from quarantine. This is a path we must all walk on our own. This is where the psychedelic experience and kundalini awakening come in. You will find at a "level 5" psychedelic experience "ego death" is common, and kundalini awakening is assisted by removal (or destruction) of ego. The ego separates us from God, and divided we fall. We are all "born" into the "physical world" with the ego-consciousness in control of the "body". The ego doesn't want to lose control of the body and it uses fear to maintain control. Do not be afraid, just let it go…

Imagine for a minute, with relaxed eyes, being within a shell, a large shell shaped like a body. In the beginning of your "awakening" you realize this is where you are and you're small and located around the pelvis area of the shell. Naturally we begin to move upwards towards the head. Moving upward, feel the unfolding of energy from within. As we focus and progress through the chakra gates up, we find the last gate to open, the thousand petal lotus, and the illusion of "death". It is this very illusion that guards the door to immortality and enlightenment. After overcoming the fear of death by surrendering to it, the final gate opens and a full transcendental awakening is achieved. A fully awakened one no longer thinks (*suffers*) with the physical mind and its limitations, rather the kundalini ("*God's child*") operates the body (*pursuing the spiritual goal (divine will) free from distraction*) in order to free others as it has been freed.

The only thing that matters to me, now that I have awakened, is to save your life. How will I save your life, you might ask? I will save you as God saved me, by showing you the truth. The truth is that we are all already "born" "dead" from birth. We are all dead in this "world of the dead" because we are each born with a dormant kundalini, with the ego-consciousness in control. This "dormant" kundalini (*the real you*) is simply a seed of God's consciousness. To an immortal being, unconsciousness, (*or dormancy*) is as dead as it gets. In this dormant state, we act as merely a battery which powers the body. We are slaves to the body, as a battery is a slave to what it powers. The body (*your vessel which you power*) has its own preprogrammed insatiable physical desires ("*sins*") which constantly distract our attention and constantly try to get us to expend our energy on pursuing its desires. Only by identifying those desires as they are can one become strong against their distractions. Only once you've overcome the desires and influences "*of the flesh*", can you learn to focus on your one true spiritual goal, fully awakening (*spiritual consciousness= heaven*), and then awakening others.

The most important thing to remember is: to be physical is to be "dead". Only by overcoming the desire to remain physical, can one hope to overcome death. "Escape" "the World", your "life" depends on it. We are all in "Heaven" right now; we are just unconscious of it. God (*our spiritual father*) wants us all to simply "wake up".

I have now passed on to you the key to unlocking the simple truth, what you choose to do with it is up to you.

Good Luck!

Sean Williams, instrument

Going to "Heaven", the Practical Approach

1. What is "Heaven"?

Heaven, Enlightenment, Nirvana, these are all different names to describe the same understanding. A final blessed state, free from ignorance, desire, and suffering. "Heaven" to a battery is to be free of that which drains its energy. "Heaven" is in actuality a state of full spiritual consciousness. It is to; exist without the body, in a state of pure transcendental consciousness.

2. What is "Hell"?

Hell is spiritual unconsciousness. It is to be used as a battery to power the body with no spiritual will power to control it. To be trapped in a body controlled by the ego-consciousness. Ironically we choose to be in the unconscious (battery) state. It is a choice we are unaware of, yet we make it still because it is what the ego desires.

3. Is there a "God" and a "Devil"?

The simple answer is yes, but not in the forms that many people picture them. God and the devil are both within each of us. The devil is the (egotistic material self) that is only focused on "me" or "I". God is the energetic love that flows from us which is concerned only with the helping of others. To return to "God" is to return to a state of pure bliss and love completely devoid of the ego which causes suffering.

4. Energy?

Any doctor can tell you that it takes energy to make our muscles contract, but their explanations get vague after that. Well, I can tell you that you are not the muscles or the body, but the "true you" is the energy. It is this energy that is a child of God. Sadly, as we are all "born" into the material world, our true self (energy) is "born" in an "unconscious" condition in which our true potential is reduced to that of a battery to power the egotistical material self (physical body).

5. **What is the "body"?**

The body is a vessel which comes "pre-programmed" with basic commands which are in place to insure the continuation of "life" in "the world". These "bodies" when limited to their basic programming are easy to control and influence. Only through "awakening" can one begin to get control of their vessel and overcome its insatiable physical desires.

6. **What is "Sin"?**

As I said before our bodies come "pre-programmed". Well "Sin" in its simplest form are these "pre-programmings" and our desire to satisfy those desires which are insatiable (physical desire). The term "Original Sin" comes from the choice which was made to experience physical life in the beginning. This is what most canonical religions mean when they talk of repentance of sin, but because they do not themselves have a clear understanding, they cannot help you form your own understanding. Ultimately "Sin" comes down to you giving in "to the will of the flesh", as Jesus would say.

7. **Physical Pre-programming?**

Ok, scientists call it, Genetics, DNA; basically it's the blue print for the continuation of the world of physical existence. Without the "will of the flesh" (Physical desires) "Life" as we know it cannot continue. Survival itself is one of the most basic physical desires, which creates eating, drinking, and procreation desires. "Society" has become comfortable by helping you temporarily satisfy those desires which are insatiable, and most "give in" to without much thought. Society itself has created its own unnecessary insatiable physical desires such as wealth, power, vanity, fame, leisure, prosperity, comfort, just to name a few. These are programmed after birth through various methods, TV, radio, public and private schools. These desires are those which don't have a point of fulfillment, you can never get enough and can waste your entire life trying to attain the unattainable. Just trying to constantly satisfy those insatiable desires for an entire lifetime seems a bit like hell to me. If we add in the reincarnation (or rebirth) aspect, then one could understand eternity in hell, a hell we are all in by choice. Overcome your physical pre-programming, become strong against "the world" of distraction, focus.

8. **Choices**

Every moment of every day we are making choices. We are making choices pertaining to which one of the base physical desires we devote our power to. We devote power by allowing our attention to dwell on those desires. With all of the necessary and unnecessary physical desires fighting for attention, society only needs to suggest that we "need" things for many of us to succumb to "temptation" and divert our power away from where we should be focusing it, to go "into the world" to suffer and attain. Ultimately we even make the choice of whether or not we want to go to "heaven". At the end of our physical lives, if we still desire to remain physical and "in the world", then that is where we will stay. Although if we were courageous and humble enough to use the entheogenic "keys of knowledge" to feel the blissful state that awaits beyond "the world" and the joy of liberation from the physical desire we all experience during our "physical lives", then when we are faced with the choice of which type of consciousness we want, we will be better prepared to make that choice.

9. When is it time to let go?

Letting go.... This seems to be a common reoccurring message that turns up in many movies and video games, also in religion it is referred to as "surrendering". In "Finding Nemo", "Dori" tells "Marlon" to just "let go" when "Marlon" was afraid because he perceived he was about to be eaten by a whale, but by "letting go" they were able to continue their journey to completion, without "letting go" they would have failed and been digested. In "The Matrix", "Morpheus" speaks of "letting go" when he is teaching "Neo" about saving the people still trapped in the illusionary world of "The Matrix", and how many people have trouble doing it. This is what entheogens like magic mushrooms teach, how to "let go". They teach how to let go of the physical consciousness of suffering in order to evolve into a spiritual consciousness without suffering. To have physical desire is to suffer. "God" will not take it from you if you won't let it go.

10. What is the "goal" of "life"?

To understand this takes a quite a bit of deep meditation. Through my meditation, I've come to understand the "goal" of "life" to be, to gain liberation from "the body". During what we perceive as "our lives", we are meant to grow spiritually. During our conception (when mommy and daddy got together and "we" were "created") there was a merging of energy and matter. At this point, the energy (our true self) was not strong enough to exist without the "matter" (the physical body acts as a cradle to keep the energy safe so it can grow). Again "the body" comes pre-programmed with the basic commands required to maintain life. In the beginning we are simply not strong enough to overcome these "pre-programmings". So we succumb to the will of the flesh and then just get used to it. The goal of "life" is then easy to understand, first and foremost, overcome the basic physical desires so that you can focus on your spiritual goal. Understand secondly that our spiritual goal (growth) is the most important goal, with the optimum outcome being to outgrow the body and become a being of pure energy. Ultimately this path leads one to understand the mortality of the physical self, and to the ultimate decision of letting the body and "the world", go away.

11.   We have been given "tools" to assist us.

Entheogens are those tools. The Wikipedia definition of an entheogen ("creates God within") is a psychoactive substance used in a religious, shamanic or spiritual context. Entheogens are tools to supplement various practices for healing and transcendence, including in meditation, psychonautics, art projects, and psychedelic therapy. Most entheogens do not produce drug dependency. Entheogens have been described as "Mystic Communion" and because of their potential to unite "God" and man; their true purpose has been hidden by organized religion and government who seeks to control us as slaves. Ultimately, organized religion teaches us about "their" understanding of "heaven" which is based on theory, whereas entheogens specifically allow us to temporarily experience "heaven" so that when it is time for us to make the choice to "go there" (wake up), we know what to expect and fear doesn't prevent us. In short, Entheogens teach us how to "die" which is the one thing we must learn to do before "going to heaven", which organized religion fails to teach.

12.   What is Humanity?

Humanity is simply just another step in the evolution of our consciousnesses in which we are all meant to achieve specific understandings required to continue on to our next step. One of the understandings is indeed learning to "let go" of the "step" we are all on now, so that we can be ready to move on to the next "step". Humanity is society as a whole. It is generally physical thought itself, based solely on pursuing the needs of the "body's" desires, and the civilization that has arisen from the system designed to profit from you being controlled by the desires "of the body". Humanity is impurity of the spiritual self. To completely let go of one's Humanity, is to achieve "spiritual perfection", and enlightenment.

13. Enlightenment?

To understand "enlightenment", is to know "Heaven". Enlightenment is an understanding of all things. I have come to understand that there are different levels of "enlightenment", which range from becoming "aware" of subtle subliminal "messages" and clues sown into the very fabric of society and "reality" as we perceive it in the beginning, to the rare level of one who is able to completely understand the "messages" to the point that they can use them to help guide others along their paths to enlightenment. The Wikipedia describes "Enlightenment" as, "A final blessed state, free from ignorance, desire, and suffering". The Wikipedia also confirms that during a "level 5" psychedelic experience, "many people experience religious phenomenon. Often mentioned are an "all-powerful presence" or a "universal knowledge", which many equate to their idea of "God" or "Enlightenment".

14. Want to "Go to"... "Heaven"?

Ok now, understand first that "heaven" is not a place. Since it is not a place, one cannot "go" there. Rather, it is a shift in the nature of one's consciousness to the point that it is no longer sullied by the taint of matter. It is to be free of the body. The physical world is the "waiting room" for "heaven", when you are called, don't fight it. This is what entheogens do, they allow one to experience temporarily what happens when you and your body separate so that you can get used to it. ("Out of body" experiences are common during psychedelic experiences) The truth is, no one can tell you "how" to "go to heaven", but that doesn't mean it doesn't need to be learned. I learned by eating psilocybin mushrooms. I understand that just because I understand, it doesn't mean that I can explain it to you in a way that would make you understand. Words seem to fall short when trying to describe the feeling of "heaven". The only true way for you to understand is to experience that which I experienced for yourself. Learning to ride a bike in theory, isn't the same as getting on, putting your feet on the peddles and feeling it. You can't explain to someone who hasn't ridden a bike, what the feeling is like, because they don't have the experience to relate too. Only by helping them experience riding the bike for themselves, can you truly share the feeling, and it is the same with "going to heaven" after eating "shrooms" (or other entheogens).

All My Research

I've done quite a bit of research to support the theories presented in this book. To try and place all of the information that I've researched into this book, would make the book so large that you would have a hard time just lifting it, much less reading it. So instead, I'm going to pinpoint the subjects that I researched and quote only the information that I found beneficial to this theory. I would recommend though that individual, more extensive research into each individual subject be done. Learn all you can. Knowledge is power. The truth will set you free...

Much of my research comes from "The Wikipedia", an extensive free "on-line" encyclopedia. With any of these individual subjects, much more information can be found by simply "logging on" and reading. Use the "related topics" section to help guide your way.

Mysticism – is the pursuit of communion with, identity with, or conscious awareness of an ultimate reality, divinity, spiritual truth, or God through direct experience, intuition, or insight. Mysticism usually centers on a practice or practices intended to nurture that experience or awareness. "Enlightenment" or "Illumination" are generic English terms for the phenomenon which were adopted from English translations of Buddhist texts, but used loosely to describe the state of mystical attainment regardless of "faith". The term "mysticism" is used to refer to beliefs and practices which go beyond the liturgical and devotional forms of worship of mainstream faith, often by seeking out inner or esoteric meanings of conventional religious doctrine. Mystics hold that there is a deeper or more fundamental state of existence beneath the observable, day-to-day world of phenomena, and that in fact the ordinary world is superficial or epiphenomenal. In some cases – Christianity, Buddhism, Mosaic law...- entire non-mystical (doctrine based) faiths have arisen around the teachings of individuals who are considered to have special mystical insight, with few or no mystical practitioners remaining. Hinduism has many mystical sects in part due to its historic reliance on gurus (individual teachers of insight) for transmission of its philosophy. Mysticisms generally hold to some form of immanence, since their focus on direct realization obviates many concerns about the afterlife, and this often conflicts with conventional religious doctrines. Mystical teachings are passed down through transmission from teacher to student, generally only once the student has been deemed "ready", will the processes and practices be revealed. Upon which time the "teacher" becomes merely a "guide", aiding the student in the process, allowing the plant to do the teaching. Mystics may make use of canonical and non-canonical religious texts, and will generally interpret them hermeneutically, developing a philosophical perspective distinct from conventional religious interpretations. Vivekananda in Vedanta, for instance, is noted for his assertions that all religions are one. As a rule mystics are less concerned with religious differences and more concerned with social or individual development.

Evelyn Underhill has identified five stages of the process by which the mystic arrives at union with the absolute. First is the "awakening", the stage in which one begins to have some consciousness of absolute or divine reality. The second stage is one of "purgation" which is characterized by an awareness of one's own imperfections and finiteness. The response in this stage is one of self-discipline and mortification. The third stage is one reached by artists and visionaries as well as being the final stage of some mystics. It is marked by a consciousness of a transcendent order and a vision of a new heaven and a new earth. Very few go beyond to the fourth stage which is one of final and complete purification. It is the period of final "unselfing" and the surrender to the hidden purposes of the divine will. The final and last stage is one of "union with the object of love, the one reality, God. Here the self has been permanently established on a transcendental level and liberated for a new purpose. Filled up with the divine will, it immerses itself in the temporal order, the world of appearances in order to incarnate the eternal in time, to become the mediator between humanity and eternity.

The mystic interprets the world through a different lens than is present in ordinary experience, their sayings simultaneously over-simplified and full of subtle meanings hidden from the un-enlightened. References to "the world" are common in mystical and religious traditions including admonitions to be separate and the call to detachment which is analogous to emptiness. "The world" of appearances reflects only learned beliefs- based on the limitations of time, culture, and relationships- and that unquestioned faith in those misperceptions limits one's return to the divine state. The cloaking of such insights to the uninitiated is an age-old tradition; the malleableness of reality was thought to pose a significant danger to those harboring impurities.

Christ is well known for his use of parables, consistently using them to teach compassion and inclusion, while many contain hidden metaphorical content for "those who have ears to hear". In the Gospel of Thomas (114 sayings by the living Jesus) each word of the document has significance in describing the return path to the divine through a gradual emptying of earthbound value concepts and subtle internal conflicts. The blatant old woman carrying all she values (a bag of grain) is a common metaphor related to the mind's creative incapacity when controlled by blatant ego values.

Mysticism is generally considered experiential and holistic, and mystical experiences held to be beyond expression (ineffable). Plato and Pythagoras, and to a lesser extent Socrates, had clear mystical elements in their teachings. Socrates was deemed a "heretic" and forced to drink hemlock (poison) or abandon his values and teachings and pay a fine to the church. He drank the poison and gladly died for what he believed in.

Physicist David Bohm speaking of consciousness expressing itself as matter and/ or energy would be completely understood by the mystic, whatever his cultural/ religious heritage. The mystic's pursuit of emptiness-despite its fear producing angst- for the sake of union with the Divine, points directly toward a potential unity between physics and psychology that does not at present exist.

Every mystical path has necessarily as its ontological purpose, the discernment between truth and illusion, and many approaches emphasize the total disregarding of beliefs as the prerequisite to receiving knowledge in the phenomenological sense. The focus of these "paths" is generally in finding practices which will yield clear perception. The mystics awareness of evolving levels of consciousness encompass another realm altogether.

"Of course, if you haven't awakened to cognition (this understanding), then you will see none of this, just as a rock cannot see mental images. And you will probably have unpleasant things to say about people who do see them". Spiritual transcendence and religion have little in common. That we are shaped by the culture we create makes it difficult to see that our culture is what must be transcended, which means we must rise above our notions and techniques of survival itself, if we are to survive. Thus the paradox, that only as we lose our life, do we find it."

Goals sought and reasons for seeking mystical experience- Theistic, pantheistic, and panentheistic metaphysical systems most often understand mystical experience as individual communion with a God. One can receive these very subjective experiences as visions, miracles, dreams, revelations, or prophecies, for example. Going beyond "natural theology" to direct experience of God is "mystical theology" or, as Thomas Aquinas defined it, "experiential knowledge of God". Repentance (awareness of lower-self attachments) and ascetics (giving up the thoughts/behaviors) is the requirement for reestablishing divine communion/unity/grace.

Enlightenment is becoming aware of the nature of the self through observation. By examination of the interior thought system and emotions with detachment, one becomes aware of its processes without being controlled by them, allowing one greater creative capacity and ease of interaction with others and the environment. Once the "potentiality" of "the experience" has been experienced/received/observed, understanding how and why it has occurred becomes the goal of the individual and permanently stabilizing this "direct experience of God" is obsessively perused. It is extremely difficult for anyone, who has not experienced the simultaneity of the "shift in awareness/reality" to translate mystical language in a useful way.

Some see the learned self (material self as opposed to essence) as wicked and deserving of punishment or extreme neglect through asceticism, with positive values placed only upon the transcendent true self. The Jainist view of soul is perceivable non-matter which has the ability to connect to infinite knowledge but cannot receive that knowledge without removal of the blanket of karma, but as self knowledge is gained, the hold of karma is loosened, everything can be seen clearly and nirvana (salvation) is achieved. The pure soul- divine unity- is accomplished when all the power of karma is destroyed. In Islam the mystical path incorporated within Sufi and the Self/Soul is embattled (jihad) with the infidel/ego. Eastern philosophies, such as Hinduism, Buddhism, and Taoism are concerned with the individual soul's dissolution of ego into transcendent reality. Hindu mystical practices aim for "God-consciousness" and the loss of the lower self. Buddhist teaching holds that all suffering in the world comes from craving, aversion and ignorance, and that freedom from suffering comes from the extinction of these poisons which are the source of mental defilements, through the developments of insight and equanimity. Acosmism denies the reality of the universe, seeing it as ultimately illusory (Maya), with only the infinite unmanifest Absolute as real. There are also dualist conceptions, often with an evil (though existent) material world of the ego, competing with a transcendent and perfect spiritual plane aligned with the true self/essence.

Gnosticism is a term for various mystical initiatory religions, sects and knowledge schools which were most active in the first few centuries of the Christian/Common Era. These systems typically recommend the pursuit of special knowledge (gnosis) as the central goal of life. They also commonly depict creation as a dualistic struggle between competing forces of light and dark, and posit a marked division between the material realm, which is typically depicted as under the governance of malign forces, and the higher spiritual realm from which it is divided. As a result of these traits, dualism, anticosmism and body-hatred are sometimes present within Gnosticism.

Ramesh Balsekar comments on nonduality and mysticism. "Consciousness-at-rest is not aware of Itself only the force around it. It becomes aware of Itself only when this sudden feeling, "I-am", arises, the impersonal sense of being aware. And that is when Consciousness-at-rest becomes Consciousness-in-movement, Potential energy becomes actual energy. They are not two. Nothing separate comes out of Potential energy becoming the one true being...That moment that science calls the Big Bang, the mystic calls the sudden arising of awareness..."

Related to syncretism, Mystics of different traditions report similar experiences of a world/reality outside conventional perception, although this does not infer an abandonment of knowledge through normal means (non-entheogenic research). Mystics describe the same unity experience across history, culture and religion – despite the extreme individuality of the experience. If the attempt of religion, philosophy and science to describe reality is comparative to the fable of five blind men attempting to define an elephant by describing its parts, the mystic of every religion and culture sees the elephant despite the individuality of approach and differences in culture and language. *Elements of mysticism exist at the core of all religions and in many philosophies, including those where the majority of the followers have no awareness of this. Some mystics perceive a common thread of divine influence in all religions and philosophies.* The Vedic tradition is inherently mystic; the Christian apocalyptic Book of Revelation is clearly mystical, as with Ezekiel's or Daniel's visions of Judaism, and Muslims believe that the angel Gabriel revealed the Qur'an in a miraculous manner. Indigenous cultures also have cryptic revelations pointing toward a universal love or unity, usually following a vision quest or similar ritual.

Most mystical paths arise in the context of some particular religion but tend to set aside or move beyond these institutional structures, often believing themselves to be following the 'purest' or 'deepest' representations of that faith. The mystic's disregard of religious institutional structures often lends a quasi-revolutionary aspect to mystical teaching, and this occasionally leads to conflict with established religious and political structures, or the creation of splinter groups or new faiths.

Some mystics use the term "perennial philosophy" to refer to a manner wherein the mystic strives to plumb the depths of the self and reality in a radical process of meditative self exploration, with the aim of experiencing the true nature of reality. In some cultures and traditions, mind-altering substances – often referred to as entheogens – have been used as a guide; the Uniao de Vegetal being a notable modern example.

And this leads us to... Entheogens...

Entheogen – An entheogen ("creates god within"), in the strict sense, is a psycho active substance used in a religious, shamanic or spiritual context. Historically, entheogens were mostly derived from (natural) plant sources and have been used in a variety of traditional religious contexts. Most entheogens do not produce drug dependency. Entheogens are "tools" to supplement various "practices" for healing and transcendence, including in meditation, psychonautics, art projects, and psychedelic therapy.

More broadly, the term entheogen is used to refer to any psychoactive substances when used for their religious or spiritual effects, whether or not in a formal religious or traditional structure. Spiritual effects of psychedelic compounds have been demonstrated scientifically, though current research is limited due to drug prohibition. Some of the more commonly recognized of these substances are known as "Weed" (cannabis), "Shrooms" or "magic mushrooms" (psilocybe mushrooms), "peyote", "Salvia Divinorum", and that's just to name a few. Essentially all psychoactive drugs, especially psychedelics, dissociatives and deliriants, can be used in an entheogenic context, although, psilocybe mushrooms are the most commonly used.

Although entheogens are taboo and most of them are officially prohibited in Christian and Islamic societies, their ubiquity and prominence in the spiritual traditions of various other cultures is unquestioned. Most of the well-known modern examples, such as peyote, psilocybe and other psychoactive mushrooms, are from the native cultures of the Americas. The Indo-Europeans brought with them the knowledge of the wild amanita mushroom. It could not be cultivated; thus it had to be found (in the wilderness), which suited it to a nomadic lifestyle.

With psilocybe cubensis mushrooms, the entheogen is now easily cultivable. Entheogens are divine food. They are not something to be sampled lightly, not something to be profaned. It was the food of the gods, their ambrosia, and it mediated between the two realms. The entheogen is believed to offer godlike powers in many traditional tales, including immortality.

The philologist John Marco Allegro has suggested that the self-revelation and healing abilities attributed to the figure of Jesus may have been associated with the effects of the plant medicines. Merkur contends that a minority of Christian hermits and mystics could possibly have used entheogens, in conjunction with fasting, meditation and prayer. Allegro was the only "non-Catholic" appointed to the position of translating the Dead Sea scrolls. His extrapolations (translations) are often the subject of scorn due to Allegro's non-mainstream theory of Jesus as a mythological personification of the essence of a "psychoactive sacrament"; furthermore they conflict with the position of the Catholic Church and the use of the sacramental bread and wine, which do not contain psychoactive substances.

Naturally occurring entheogens such as psilocybin and DMT were, for the most part, discovered and used by older cultures, as part of their spiritual and religious life, as plants and agents which were respected, or in some cases revered for generations and may be a tradition which predates all modern religions as a sort of proto-religious rite. They have been used in various ways, including as part of established religions, secularly for personal spiritual development as tools (or "plant teachers") to augment the mind.

Many various entheogens have been used by various indigenous cultures from every continent since before the growth of Roman Christianity which also saw the end of the two-thousand-year-old tradition of the Eleusinian Mysteries. Natives of Papua New Guinea are known to use several species of entheogenic mushrooms. Many books have been written which infer importance to the use of entheogenic mushrooms and other plants such as the mushroom consumed in the book "The Transmigration of Timothy Archer" in which the consuming the mushroom preceded the birth of Christianity. A theme inspired by John Allegro's book.

This brings us to Entheogenic drugs and the archaeological record...

ENTHEOGENIC DRUGS AND THE ARCHAEOLOGICAL RECORD.

There are several modern cultures that continue to practice the application of mind-altering drugs for religious purposes. Some of these cultures include the Shamans of Siberia (who employ fly agarics to induce hallucinations), the Huichol Indians of Mexico (who use peyote cactus), and the Rastafarians of the Caribbean (who use marijuana).

Mesoamerican entheogenic drug use is the most iconic in popular consciousness. The Maya, Olmecs, and Aztecs have well-documented entheogenic complexes. North American cultures, too, have long-established traditions of entheogens. The Olmecs are largely viewed as the mother culture of the Aztecs and Maya. The Maya flourished in Central America and were prevalent until the arrival of the Spanish. The Maya religion displays characteristic Mesoamerican mythology, with a strong emphasis on an individual being a communicator between the physical world and the spiritual world. Mushroom stone effigies, dated to 700 CE, give evidence that mushrooms were at least revered in a religious way. The most direct evidence of Maya entheogen use comes from modern descendents of the Maya who use entheogenic drugs today. The Aztecs used several entheogenic plants and referred to psilocybe mushrooms as "Teonanacatl" (translated as "Mushroom of the Gods").

ENTHEOGENIC DRUGS AND MAJOR WORLD RELIGIONS

There have been several reports stating that the Bible and the Vedas have several references to entheogenic drugs.

MANNA AND MUSHROOMS

Some researchers speculate that Manna, the food that the Israeli tribes harvest, was actually an entheogenic drug. The Bible is quoted in Exodus 16:14 reads:

"And when the dew that lay was gone up, behold, upon the face of the wilderness there lay a small round thing, as small as the hoarfrost on the ground. And when the children of Israel saw it, they said to one another, It is Manna: for they wist not what it was. And Moses said unto them, This is the bread which the Lord hath given you to eat."

Some point to the similarities of psilocybe mushrooms and the biblical description of manna as evidence.

This brings us to the Psychedelic Experience...

PSYCHEDELIC EXPERIENCE

A psychedelic experience is the name given to describe what happens when one consumes an entheogenic compound, such as psilocybe mushrooms among others. A psychedelic experience is characterized by the perception of aspects of one's mind previously unknown, or by the creative exuberance of the mind once liberated from its ordinary restraints. Literally it means "Soul Manifestation".

The psychedelic experience is an intimate experience, but there are many common themes in the various descriptions of the experience, which range from a sense of connectedness to everything in the immediate vicinity, to a sense of oneness with everything in the universe. Potentially, the range of the drug-induced psychedelic experience goes far beyond drugs. For many, such experiences come to be seen as personal re-enactments of a hero's journey. Spiritual practices and Psychedelic drugs can be used as a means to achieve states of mind in which novel perceptions can arise, unhindered by everyday mental filters and processes. The mental and emotional impact of the experience is positive and enduring for many.

Erowid has contributed greatly to the cause of proving the importance of the entheogens role in guiding society, by forming a vast library of subjects related to entheogenics and the psychedelic experience in general. The five level scale they use to describe the psychedelic experience is an excellent representation of putting something so profoundly beautiful into words which intrigue the mind, but fail to give complete understanding, without the actual experience from which to draw upon required to understand. Their description is gathered from decades of studying many people who have experienced psilocybin mushrooms among the other entheogens, and was derived by compiling and comparing the different versions to form the common thread. The description follows:

LEVELS OF PSYCHEDELIC EXPERIENCE

The Psychedelic Experience FAQ (http://www.erowid.org/psychoactives/faqs/psychedelic_experience_faq.shtml) describes five different levels of psychedelic experience acquired by substances and chemicals:

LEVEL 1

This level produces a mild "high" effect, with some visual enhancement (e.g. brighter colors) and music sounds "wider", or more piercing to the ears. There is a sense that one's thoughts are spiraling into themselves. This level can be achieved from a normal dose of cannabis or a very low dose of a classic psychedelic such as psilocybin. Occasionally common prescription drugs like SSRIs can produce mild "trippy" effects, as well, through they are not normally classified as psychedelic experiences because they are so mild.

LEVEL 2

Bright colors; visuals (e.g. things may appear to move or breath); some two-dimensional patterns become apparent upon shutting eyes. Confused, cyclic (thought loop) or reminiscent thoughts. Déjà vu is commonly reported. Change in short term memory leads to continually distracting thought patterns. While it may become increasingly difficult to follow a single train of thought, at other times one might find themselves lost in deep introspection about one specific idea or problem. The need to see 'normal' reality becomes less, the urge to venture 'beyond the void' becomes more. Level 3 tripping can intersperse with level 2 as long as eyes are shut. This state can be achieved from higher doses of cannabis or a low dose of psilocybin or LSD.

LEVEL 3

Very obvious visuals, everything looking curved and/or warped, patterns, kaleidoscopes or fractal images seen on walls, landscapes, faces, etc. Closed eye hallucinations become three dimensional. There is some confusing of the senses (synesthesia). One can experience "time distortions" and "moments of eternity". Movement at times becomes extremely difficult. A normal dose of either psilocybin or LSD can produce this state.

LEVEL 4

Strong visual effects (e.g. objects morphing into other objects). Dissolving or multiple splitting of the ego (e.g. things start talking, "burning bush", or feeling of contradictory things simultaneously). The loss of sense of self can bring a shift in the sense of reality, often accompanied by a sense of ineffable lucidity (abstract clarity, and an understanding of subjects not usually thought about, which is difficult to relate to others). Time becomes very distorted and participants may perceive an activity lasting only minutes to have encompassed hours of their own reality (or vice versa) (similar to your whole life flashing before you in the last moment before you "die"). Out-of-body experiences and mystical visions are common at this level. A high dose of psilocybin or LSD can produce this effect, as can a normal dose of Salvia divinorum.

LEVEL 5

Total loss of visual connection with reality (A scene similar to in the movie "The Matrix" after "Neo" swallows the red pill, or a complete spiritual awakening). The senses cease to function in the normal way. One may feel like they are merging with space, other objects, or the universe, or feel oneness with the world. There are powerful, and sometimes brutal, psycho-physical reactions interpreted by some users as reliving their own birth. Feelings of reaching to the beginning or the end of space and time. The loss of reality becomes so extreme that it becomes ineffable (understood by the experiencer, but impossible to relate to others in words). Dream or movie-like states, people have reported seeing themselves in entirely different settings than their original setting.

Many people experience religious phenomenon at this level. Often mentioned are an "all-powerful presence" or a "universal knowledge", which many equate to their idea of God or enlightenment.

Earlier levels are relatively easy to describe in terms of measureable changes in perception and thought patterns. "Ego loss", or complete dissolution of one's awareness of the existence of Self, (the separation of your spiritual self, from your physical self) is an essential trait of level 5 experiences; the boundaries between "self" and encompassing reality cease to exist, and all that one is conscious of, is the abstract manifestations of the hallucination (the spirit world). Thoughts are not processed or realized in words or an "inner voice", as in everyday life; in the midst of a level 5 hallucination, it is essentially impossible to distinguish conscious thought from the hallucination itself. This feeling has been described, with Tryptamine-based hallucinogens like LSD or high doses of psilocybin, as a sense of "oneness" with the universe; with extremely powerful entheogens such as DMT or salvia divinorum, the resultant hallucination is difficult to describe, but has been likened by some to being "transformed into a Picasso painting".

Many people claim to have spoken to intelligent entities during their trips, to have experienced alternate dimensions (the spirit world), or to have existed for thousands of years (in spirit form on the plane of eternity) - often not as a human but as an abstract entity such as shadow or paint- though the trip itself, in the case of salvia and DMT, "the trip" lasted only five to ten minutes. This effect can be produced in high doses of LSD, Ketamine, salvia divinorum, and high doses of psilocybin. DMT is known to send people to level 5 with an average dose, making it one of the most potent and psychoactive psychedelics known to man. It occurs naturally in each one of us, it is present within our head.

This leads us to the Psychology of religion...

Psychology of religion is the psychological study of religious experiences, beliefs, and activities.

William James, a U.S. psychologist and philosopher (1842-1910) is regarded by most psychologists of religion as the founder of the field. He served as president of the American Psychological Association, and wrote one of the first psychology textbooks. In the psychology of religion, James' influence endures. His "Varieties of Religious Experience" is considered to be the classic work in the field, and references to James' ideas are common at professional conferences.

James distinguished between institutional religion and personal religion. Institutional religion refers to the religious group or organization, and plays an important part in a society's culture. Personal religion, in which the individual has mystical experience, can be experienced regardless of the culture. James was most interested in understanding personal religious experience. William James was also interested in mystical experiences from a drug-induced perspective, leading him to make some experiments with nitrous oxide and even peyote. He concludes that while the revelations of the mystic hold true, they hold true only for the mystic; for others they are certainly ideas to be considered, but hold no claim to truth without personal experience of such.

James Leuba, an American psychologist, in "A Psychological Study of Religion", accounts for Mystical experience psychologically and physiologically, pointing to analogies (similarities) with certain drug induced experiences.

The effects of meditation – The large variety of meditation techniques shares the common goal of shifting attention away from habitual or customary modes of thinking and perception, in order to permit experiencing in a different way. Many religious and spiritual traditions that employ meditation assert that the world most of us know is an illusion. This illusion is said to be created by our habitual mode of separating, classifying and labeling our perceptual experiences. Meditation is "empirical" in that it involves direct experience. Though, it is also "subjective" in that the meditative state can be directly known only by the experiencer, and may be difficult or impossible to fully describe in words. Concentrative meditation can induce an altered state of consciousness characterized by a loss of awareness of extraneous stimuli, one-pointed attention to the meditation object to the exclusion of all other thoughts, and feelings of bliss.

This leads us to Psychedelic Yoga...

Psychedelic Yoga – The Application of Yoga Meditation Techniques to the Use of Psychedelic Sacraments. The fact that psychedelic drugs induce a greater sensitivity to subtle spiritual and psychic energies, and speed up the influx of impressions from deeper levels of consciousness, raises the immediate question of how these energies can be properly understood and handled.

According to Yoga philosophy, the most spiritual and powerful aspect of a man's nature is the faculty of attention or consciousness. The most fundamental aspect of man's free will is the choice as to what he allows his attention to dwell upon. The attention always has to be on something, but we can choose what we allow it to dwell upon. The goal of all Yoga practices is to discover and directly experience what the attention or faculty of consciousness in man is. The Yogi seeks to know that principle by which all else is known. This goal is achieved by observing the observer or placing the attention on the attention itself. This may at first seem very abstract and hard to grasp in terms of practical application, but there are workable, time-proven methods for achieving this state of pure consciousness which when consistently applied and practiced are bound to yield results.

It should be constantly remembered during a psychedelic session that whatever perceptions, thoughts and even hallucinations occur, they are all the creations of one's own mind and consciousness, and are filtered through one's own instrument of perception. These perceptions are patterning's of our own psychic energy. We give energy to whatever thoughts and feelings we allow the attention to dwell upon. It becomes clear that the key to remaining in control of a psychedelic experience is in controlling the flow of attention. Distractive experiences should be avoided in the first place, and the flow of attention can be properly directed by the use of Raja Yoga techniques of meditation. A few of these forms are known as, Chakra based meditation, such as Sound Current Meditation, Meditation on the light in the head, and Meditation on the Chakras themselves. As we begin to understand Chakras and their importance, and by concentrating the attention in the Sahasraram Chakra or "Thousand-Petalled Lotus, located at the top of the head, an experienced meditator can release an even more powerful radiation of light and spiritual energy. (It may take more work to activate this chakra) The Sahasraram Wheel is the highest chakra; called the "Doorway to the Infinite", it is the most powerful and spiritual of all the centers that can be awakened in man. When the Sahasraram Chakra is fully activated in a perfected yogin or saint, the white fire of Cosmic Kundalini descends upon him and blends with his own rising kundalini force, and the white light of spirituality radiates for miles around. When the Sahasraram Chakra is fully developed, union with God-consciousness is possible and Illumination takes place.

While the Kundalini awakening process through the use of the Sahasraram Chakra is the ultimate meditational experience, it may be difficult for the beginner, and therefore they may have more immediate results by focusing on the Agna Chakra (or "Third Eye Center"). The Agna Chakra has to do with the higher mind faculties of clairvoyance, scientific reasoning, willing and philosophical thought. Development of this chakra awakens the ability to see and regulate astral and mental forces on the superphysical level. There are seven Chakra centers of which the top three are most recommended to focus on. It is better to work with the Heart Center, the Agna Chakra, and the Sahasraram Chakra because these are the most directly related to the unfoldment of superconsciousness, and when awakened, will automatically develop the lower chakras. Once the pituitary gland is fully activated by the development of the Agna Chakra, all other glands are brought into proper chemical balance, thus helping to properly develop and raise the vibratory rate of all the lower chakras.

In Kundalini Yoga, an advanced yoga practice, concentration is done on the Muladora Chakra at the base of the spine in order to arouse the Kundalini Fire and channel it upwards through the center of the spine to activate the highest chakra, the Sahasraram, (thousand petalled lotus) at the top of the head.

MEDITATION ON THE "I AM" PRINCIPLE-

In the practice of this form of meditation, consciousness is made to dwell upon itself. When properly used and successfully practiced, this is the most powerful and highest form of meditation. While focusing in the Heart Chakra or in the Sahasraram Chakra at the crown of the head, place the attention on the attention itself. If any distractions come in the form of thoughts and perceptions of a specific nature, then immediately concentrate your attention upon that consciousness in you which is the experiencer of those thoughts and perceptions. Even the manifestation of spiritual light and sound current should be regarded in this way. The sound current and the light are merely the lower overtone manifestations of the pure consciousness upon which you are meditating. The more you hold your attention steady in concentration upon itself, the more the light, sound current, electrical sensations in the body, feelings of magnetic force, sensations of weightlessness, etc. will manifest automatically.

If however, you allow your attention to become distracted by any one of these manifestations, then you will be subject to the limitations of the thing by which you have been distracted; and the focusing of pure consciousness, possibly including the psychic manifestation which distracted your attention, will also stop. Seek ye first the kingdom of pure consciousness and all of these other psychic manifestations will be added unto you. Placing the attention on the attention itself can be done in any location in space, since pure consciousness, which is the same as God, is an omnipresent principle. Through the practice of focusing attention and the activation of the Sahasraram Chakra, the soul is then able to control the personality structure, making it a fit instrument of spiritual expression in the affairs of men. This form of meditation develops one-pointed concentration.

Since the use of psychedelic drugs stimulates the flow of a great amount of energy from higher planes into the lower planes, any thought and emotion patterns created during a psychedelic session are strongly imprinted and have a great deal of energy incorporated into their vibration structure. These thought and emotional patterns then act as powerful unconscious conditioning factors in our daily lives. It is therefore of the utmost importance that constructive imprints are made during a psychedelic session. Remaining in control of the attention can ensure this. In this regard, I would like to give a few final points of advice. Try not to focus the attention from one thing to another too quickly. Stay with a thought or meditation process until it is complete. Don't panic if frightening visions or hallucinations occur. Fear will make you concentrate on them all the more and thus feed them with the power of your attention. Remain detached and place your attention on that consciousness in you which is experiencing the hallucinations. Remember at all times that God exists in you in the form of your own power of attention and that power when properly directed, will control all lesser forces.

It is believed by some researchers that psychedelic drugs stimulate the secretion process of the pineal and pituitary glands, which are known by yogis and occultists to be related to the Sahasraram and the Agna chakras (which are also called the Thousand-Petalled Lotus and the Third Eye Center). This stimulation increases the flow of energy between the etheric body and the physical body. The increased vibratory rate of the astral body requires a stepped-up activity and increased vibratory rate in the mental body. This, in turn, more fully tunes the mental body in to the power, love and wisdom of the soul. Thus, an alignment of the whole being on all planes is facilitated, and a more rapid exchange of pattern imprints and energy between the various octaves or planes of energy takes place.

During the psychedelic experience, not only is the love, wisdom, and power of the soul brought to bare in the life of the personality, but the fine organization of the physical body, the etheric, astral, and mental bodies, which have been produced by the evolutionary process, are harmonically reflected and preserved in the soul.

While the physical body is the least permanent, the densest and composed of the substance of the lowest plane, it is in terms of evolution, the newest and most highly organized in terms of structure. Therefore a complete replica of it made out of the energy substance of the subtle planes, is an evolutionary gain for the soul and subtle bodies. When the physical body is sufficiently vivified by the influx of energy from the higher dimensions, it begins to create higher overtone reflections of itself in the akasha or energy substance of the higher planes, and thus its pattern is preserved and made immortal.

Therefore, when properly used, psychedelic drugs help to speed up the evolutionary process. When man has evolved to superman, he will, under the direction of the superconscious mind in accordance with God's will as it manifests in evolution, take an active part in the molding and directing of the evolution of the mineral, vegetable, and animal kingdoms.

This brings us to **Kundalini Awakening**

Kundalini – is a concentrated form of prana or life force, lying dormant in our bodies. Traditionally it is conceptualized as a coiled up serpent. It has also been described as, "a concentrated field of intelligent, cosmic invisible energy absolutely vital to life; beginning in the base of the spine as a man or woman begins to evolve in their first incarnation; fed by the chakras along the spine and by the cosmic energy entering through the feet from the earth; as wisdom is earned in each incarnation, this electromagnetic, ultrapotent energy moves slowly upward through the spine; it is directed by the speed of the soul mind as the soul-mind meets the requirements of each chakra, according to the needs and thinking of the individual; eventually this energy is unspiralled through the medulla oblongata, pituitary gland, pineal gland and through the crown chakra to unite with the silver cord; at which point, one will ascend to the higher realms to finish evolutionary cycle...

However since the concept of kundalini is almost inseparable from that of the Chakras and Shakti, a basic understanding of both is essential to understanding kundalini.

Chakras – Chakra is the Sanskrit word for wheel. Bodily Chakras are often depicted as circles, spaced at intervals along the spine. Ancient Indian tradition holds that there are seven Chakras, or energy centers. (*I've come to understand them as "gates" or "tumblers" in a "locking system". Only once they are "opened" or "aligned" can the energy of the individual reconnect with that which we have been separated. As more of the chakras are pierced or aligned, a better understanding of the divine will is achieved.*)

Chakras are a part of the ancient belief system associated with yoga. These traditions were handed down orally for thousands of years before being codified by Patanjali in his Yoga Sutras, several centuries before Christ. Chakras are energy centers which are difficult to pinpoint, but it is possible that they have some base in fact. Contemporary spiritual literature often notes that the chakras, as described in the esoteric kundalini documents, bear a strong similarity in location and number to the major endocrine glands, as well as nerve bundles called ganglions.

According to the ancient yoga system of India, Chakras play a very important part of the human energy system. The goddess Kundalini is said to awaken and unfold each chakra as she ascends through the spine, ensuring the free flow of life energy (prana or qi) throughout the body, thus balancing the chakras and promoting general health and well-being. When she has risen to the crown chakra, located at the top of the skull (associated with elevated spiritual consciousness), then all chakras have been opened and a person is said to experience enlightenment.

Anne Lewis (one of Australia's most respected Yoga teachers) remarks, "...Centuries ago, the Yoga masters realized that the human being consisted of more than just the physical body; they believed that the physical, mental, emotional and spiritual aspects of the individual were inter-related. The masters also believe that the spinning vortexes of energy overlap and correspond to various physical organs and glands and that these chakras can be regulated and harmonized, resulting in unleashing of an individual's full potential of health, happiness and spiritual awareness. When a chakra is closed, the life force energy or prana cannot travel through that part of the body. If this is the case, you may feel a lack in your life in its related area: for example, the throat chakra relates to communication. Therefore if it is blocked or closed, communication is difficult... and one may have a hard time communicating to others their feelings, beliefs, faiths and ideas.

Shakti – The term "Shakti" is very popular today, but it is usually misunderstood. Shakti can be understood by thinking about electricity. The fan will function as long as electricity powers it; the moment electricity is withdrawn, it stops working and becomes useless. The same is true of humans. We are alive as long as Shakti powers us. The moment Shakti life force withdraws, we die.

When Cosmic Energy or Universal Shakti comes into contact with Its residual Shakti, called Kundalini, hitherto lying dormant in the individual, It awakens, activating the sleeping Kundalini. The awakening of Kundalini is a sure sign of active Shakti (although even in its inactive state it still supplies the energy that keeps us alive). The individual consciously feels the oneness of one's own Shakti Kundalini with the Universal Shakti, just as a drop of water feels the union when it contacts the ocean.

How Kundalini is Awakened –

Traditionally, Kundalini energy can be awakened through three main practices: 1. Asanas (yogic postures), mudras (hand positions), and pranayama (breath-control exercises). 2. Grace of the Guru (guidance of a teacher, possibly a "plant teacher") 3. The accumulated results (spiritual growth) of devotional practices through the course of several lifetimes.

Awakening Kundalini through the grace of a guru is traditionally seen as the best and most natural way of stirring this energy. When Kundalini energy awakens through the grace of the Guru, yogic postures, mudras, and breath control exercises do not need to be performed. The second of the three practices is pretty much a shortcut to an awakened kundalini.

Author Philip St Romain says, "Kundalini energy in its pure, undifferentiated form is experienced only after the personal and pre-personal dimensions of the unconscious mind have emptied their contents. Of course, Kundalini is the energy "pushing" this cleansing process, and so the emptying of the unconscious is itself a "colored" experience of kundalini energy."

It may be said, then, that practices that facilitate the breakdown of Egoic defenses can help to awaken Kundalini. The most effective method is a combination of meditation and yogic postures such as those taught in Hatha and Raja Yoga. Also effective are certain entheogenic drug experiences, near death experiences, certain ritualized sexual practices (Tantric sex), and intensive chanting and/or dancing. If these practices only temporarily puncture the seal of repression between the conscious and unconscious mind, the kundalini energies will erupt until the repressive mechanisms are "repaired". Such an arousal, then, is short-lived in comparison with a full-blown awakening, in which at least part of the repressive seal is permanently ruptured.

Guru- A "Guru" is an individual who has experienced a full "awakening" and has decided to help others along their own journeys through a transferring of knowledge. A Guru will typically have a vast knowledge of plants, potions, and processes found useful in the spiritual healing and growth practices. Shaktipat- is a Sanskrit word in the Hindu spiritual tradition that refers to the act of a guru or spiritual teacher conferring a form of spiritual "power" or awakening on a disciple/student.

Few Christians realize that for thousands of years, Gurus have operated with gifts of healing, miracles, gifts of knowledge, and intense displays of spiritual consciousness as they stretch out and connect with a cosmic power.

The unique perspective of Siddha Mahayoga is, that because Kundalini is an intelligent force it will, upon awakening, naturally direct the practice of the student. All that is required is that, the student completely surrenders to this force. As a result of kundalini's unfoldment, spontaneous purifying movements, called kriyas will occur...

The website "Enlightened Beings" says, "Perhaps the most important thing to know and remain aware of, is that a Kundalini Awakening contains the most unbelievable expanded states of comprehension of Reality, enlightenment and absolute ecstasy. Not to mention that you've just befriended the greatest healing energy available inside you and which is extremely contagious to all human beings."

"The mere presence of a single being whose shakti is strongly active can awaken the shakti of those around him."

One does not Master Kundalini, one steps aside and allows it to do its work through you, as the vessel...

SO WHAT DOES AN AWAKENED KUNDALINI FEEL LIKE?

"A Kundalini awakening can be an experience that feels like the greatest blessing in the entire world, or the worst curse you have ever encountered. It simply depends on one thing. Whether you know that you are an infinite soul that will never die, OR you still believe you are this physical non-spiritual mortal body. Your perspective is everything when it comes to a million watts of energy pouring through you. The bigger and more inclusive your perspective is on each experience, the easier it will be for your bodymind to accept the Kundalini."

"Awakening your Kundalini can be like tapping into a million watts of electricity where your body may only have the capacity of a 100 watt bulb at the time. So you'll want to gradually prepare your bodymind so that you can open up to 100 million watts or more. Remember, this is a physical, mental, emotional and spiritual merging with the most powerful, healing, Divine, creative, sensual energy in this Universe. So you'll want to go about it slowly, respectfully and consciously."

PHYSICAL MANIFESTATIONS...

The awakened kundalini can manifest itself physically several ways, depending on "level" of awakening. Along the process of kundalini arousal, there can be extreme emotional outbursts without any apparent cause or source (laughing, crying, etc.). This is simply the effect of karma releasing.

"Kriyas" are spontaneous movements that occur after kundalini awakening. After a period when the devotee has reached a certain spiritual elevation they begin to shake, jerk, or hop or squirm uncontrollably, sometimes breaking into uncontrolled animal noises or laughter as they reach an ecstatic high. Often devotees move on to higher states of spiritual consciousness and become inert physically and appear to slip into an unconsciousness state when they lose sense of what is happening around them. This state is called "Samadhi" and it leads to a deeper spiritual experience. (like a level 5 psychedelic experience)

The ascent of the Kundalini as it pierces through the chakras is manifested in certain common physical and psychic signs. Yogis have described the trembling of the body which precedes the arousal of Kundalini. Inner sounds are sometimes heard, along with a feeling of giddiness. The Yogi visualizes a variety of forms, pure light being among the most common along with tingling sensations all over the body. The eyeballs may roll upwards or rotate; the body may bend forward or back, or even roll around on the floor. Many feel weightlessness as the mind becomes empty. The eyes may not open in spite of one's efforts to open them.

The Sakti (foundational consciousness) produces whatever experiences are necessary for the disciple's spiritual progress according to his samskaras (impression or fruit of Karmic action) or habit pattern formed by past action.

The physical effects of an awakened Kundalini vary from person to person, both in form and intensity. Not everyone will experience all or even most of these signs.

Muscle twitches, cramps or spasms. Energy rushes or immense electricity circulating the body. Itching, vibrating, prickling, tingling, stinging, or crawling sensations. Intense heat or cold. Involuntary bodily movements (found to occur more often during meditation, rest or sleep): jerking, tremors, shaking; feeling an inner force pushing one into postures or moving one's body in unusual ways. Alterations in eating and sleeping patterns. Episodes of extreme hyperactivity or, conversely, overwhelming fatigue. Intensified or diminished sexual desires. Headaches, or pressure within the skull. Racing heartbeat, pains in the chest. Digestive system problems. Numbness or pain in the limbs. Pains and blockages anywhere; often in the back and the neck. Emotional outbursts; rapid mood shifts; seemingly unprovoked or excessive episodes of grief, fear, rage, depression. Spontaneous vocalizations (including laughing and weeping)—are as unintentional and uncontrollable as hiccoughs. Hearing an inner sound or sounds, classically described as a flute, drum, waterfall, birds singing, bees buzzing, but may also sound like roaring, whooshing, or thunderous noises like ringing in the ears. Mental confusion; difficulty concentrating. Altered states of consciousness: heightened awareness; spontaneous trance states; mystical experiences. Heat, strange activity, and/or blissful sensations in the head, particularly in the crown area. Ecstasy, bliss and intervals of tremendous joy, love, peace and compassion. Psychic experiences: extrasensory perception; out of body experiences; past life memories; astral travel; astral projection; direct awareness of auras and chakras; contact with spirit guides through inner voices, dreams, or visions; healing powers. Increased creativity: new interests in self-expression and spiritual communication through music, art, poetry, etc. Intensified understanding and sensitivity: insight into one's own essence; deeper understanding of spiritual truths; exquisite awareness of one's environment (including "vibes" from others). Enlightenment experiences: direct knowing of a more expansive reality; transcendent awareness. Feelings of Union with the divine and God realization.

Kundalini has been called the most powerful force in the universe. Respect it or it will kick you to pieces. Don't seek awakening unless you are genuinely ready to turn your whole life over to your higher power, have it taken from you, and reshaped, redirected and rebuilt. "Not my Will, but Thine be done". Kundalini eats your ego based free will, and replaces it with the will of your soul. This is a door that once opened, does not close again. There is no putting the Genii back in the bottle. Surrender is the imperative of Kundalini awakening. The understanding that we each have one of these dormant energies within us gives us the realization of the potential of every human being for higher states of consciousness. St John of the Cross considered bodily ecstasy a weakness that gradually subsides in the process of transformation.

And this brings us to Shakti, and Shaktism...

Shakti – "to be able", meaning sacred force or empowerment, is the primordial cosmic energy and represents the dynamic forces that move through the entire universe. Shakti is the concept, or personification, of divine feminine creative power, sometimes referred to as "The Great Divine Mother" in Hinduism. On the earthly plane, Shakti most actively manifests through female embodiment and fertility – while also existing in males, in its potential, unmanifest form.

Not only is the Shakti responsible for creation, it is also the agent of all change. Shakti is cosmic existence as well as liberation, its most significant form being the Kundalini Shakti, a mysterious psychospiritual force. Shakti exists in a state of "svatantrya", dependence on no-one, being interdependent with the entire universe.

Shaktism – is a denomination of Hinduism that focuses worship upon Shakti or Devi the Hindu Divine Mother – as the absolute, ultimate Godhead. In the details of its philosophy and practice, Shaktism resembles Saivism. However, "Shaktas" (practitioners of Shaktism) focus most or all worship on Shakti, as the dynamic feminine aspect of the Supreme Divine. Shiva, the masculine aspect of divinity, is considered solely transcendent, and Shiva's worship is generally relegated to an auxiliary role.

Smarta Advaita – In the Smarta Advaita sect of Hinduism, Shakti is considered to be one of five equal bonafide personal forms of God.

Shakti force: Devi Prakriti – Devi Prakriti (a Shakti) in the context of Shaktis as forces, unifies Kundalini, Kriya, Itcha, Para, Jnana, and Mantrika Shaktis. Each is in a chakra.

The roots of Shaktism penetrate deep into India's prehistory. From the Goddess's earliest known appearance in Indian Paleolithic settlements more than 22,000 years ago to her subsequent resurfacing and expansion in the classical Sanskrit tradition. Shaktism has inspired great works of Sanskrit literature and Hindu philosophy. Again, Shaktas conceive the Goddess as the supreme, ultimate Godhead. She is considered to be simultaneously the source of all creation, as well as its embodiment and the energy that animates and governs it. Adi Shankara relates, "If Shiva is united with Shakti, he is able to create. If he is not, he is incapable of even stirring."

Broadly speaking, Shakti is considered to be the cosmos itself – she is the embodiment of energy and dynamism, and the motivating force behind all action and existence in the material universe. Shiva is her transcendent masculine aspect, providing the divine ground of all being. "There is no Shiva without Shakti, or Shakti without Shiva. The two in themselves are One."

Devi, in her supreme form as consciousness thus transcends gender. Indeed, this affirmation of the oneness of transcendence and immanence constitutes the very essence of the divine mother (and her) ultimate triumph. It is not, that she is infinitely superior to the male gods, but rather that she transcends her own feminine nature as Pakriti, without denying it.

Association with Tantra

A widely misunderstood concept known as "Tantra" refers to various practices of worship ranging from orthodox temple worship, to black magic and occult rituals, all the way to the western interpretations of "Tantric" ritualized sexual practices. When the tern "Tantra" is used in relation to authentic Hindu Shaktism, it most often refers to a class of ritual manuals, and – more broadly- to an esoteric methodology of Goddess-focused spiritual practice (sadhana) involving mantra, yantra, nyasa, mudra and certain elements of traditional kundalini yoga, all practiced under the guidance of a qualified guru after due initiation (diksha) and oral instruction to supplement various written sources. Within Tantric practices, all women are regarded as manifestations of Shakti, and hence they are the object of respect and devotion. Whoever offends them incurs the wrath of the great goddess. Every (male aspirant) has to realize the latent Female Principle within himself, and only by (thus) 'becoming female', is he entitled to worship the Supreme Being.

Being that Tantra is a very intimate method of worship, and one that is indescribable to anyone who has not yet experienced the beauty of it, it is a commonly identified as mumbo-jumbo by those who simply don't understand. Even among serious Hindu practitioners, It is not uncommon to encounter assertions that Shaiva and Vaishnava schools of Hinduism lead to "moksha", or spiritual liberation, whereas shaktism leads only to siddhis (occult powers) and bhukti (material enjoyments) – or, at best, to Shaivism. Such slights and misperceptions, however, are given little weight by serious Shakta theologians, who teach that each of the Divine Mother's forms is a Brahma Vidya, or path to supreme wisdom. The sadhaka of any of these goddess forms "attains ultimately, if his aspiration is such, the supreme purpose of life – Self-realization and God-realization".

"In her transcendental aspect she is Prakriti, the form of the absolute Brahman. Therefore, when we worship the Divine Mother, we are not only offering adoration to the supreme in its aspect of motherhood but also adoring the supreme absolute. She is that aspect of the supreme power by whose grace alone we shall ultimately be released from the darkness of ignorance and the bondage of Maya and taken to the abode of immortal knowledge, immortality, and bliss."

Shaktism has become a focus of some Western spiritual seekers attempting to construct new Goddess-centered faiths. An academic study of Western Kali enthusiasts noted that, "as shown in the histories of all cross-cultural religious transplants, Kali devotionalism in the West must take on its own indigenous forms if it is to adapt to its new environment". Writers and thinkers, notably feminists and participants in New Age spirituality who are attracted to goddess worship", have explored Kali in a new light. She is considered as a "symbol of wholeness and healing, associated especially with repressed female power and sexuality."

A powerful motivation behind Western interest is that many central concepts of Shaktism – including aspects of Kundalini Yoga as well as goddess worship – were once "common to the Hindu, Chaldean, Greek and Roman civilizations," but were largely lost to the West, as well as the Near and Middle East, with the rise of the Abrahamic religions:

"Of these four great ancient civilizations, working knowledge of the inner forces of enlightenment has survived on a mass scale only in India. Only in India has the inner tradition of the Goddess endured. This is the reason the teachings of India are so precious. They offer us a glimpse of what our own ancient wisdom must have been. The Indians have preserved our lost heritage. Today it is up to us to locate and restore the tradition of the living Goddess. We would do well to begin our search in India, where for not for one moment in all of human history have the children of the living Goddess forgotten their Divine Mother."

And this leads us to Near Death experiences –

I've decided to include this research because I've found that the descriptions of experiences related to near death experiences directly "mirror" the experiences described by those under clinical study of psilocybin and the psychedelic experience, along with my own feelings "of dying" (*which I have identified as "ego death"*) experienced during psychedelic sessions.

A **near-death experience (NDE)** refers to a broad range of personal experiences associated with impending death, encompassing multiple possible sensations ranging from detachment from the body, feelings of levitation, extreme fear, total serenity, security, or warmth, the experience of absolute dissolution, and the presence of a light, which some interpret as a deity. Some see NDE's as a paranormal and spiritual glimpse into the afterlife. Many NDE reports originate from events that are not life threatening. Most of the scientific community regards such experiences as hallucinatory.

The phenomenology of an NDE usually includes physiological,

psychological, and alleged transcendental aspects. Varying descriptions of experiences include, a sound or noise, a sense of being dead, pleasant emotions; calmness and serenity; out-of-body experiences; a sensation of floating above one's own body and seeing the surrounding area. Floating up a blue tunnel with a strong, bright light or garden at the end. Meeting deceased relatives or spiritual figures, encountering a being of light, or a light (often interpreted as being the deity or deities they personally believe in). Being given a life review (the "life-flashing-before-your-eyes" phenomenon); Reaching a border or boundary; A feeling of being returned to the body, often accompanied by a reluctance; and a feeling of warmth even though naked.

Some people have also experienced extremely distressing NDE's, which can manifest in forewarning of emptiness or a sense of dread towards the cessation of their life. (the psychedelic experience relates to this feeling as a "bad trip"). A "core" near-death experience encompasses peace, joy, and harmony, followed by insight and mystical or religious experiences.

Kenneth Ring (1980) subdivided the NDE on a 5 stage continuum:

1. Feelings of peace and contentment, 2. A sense of detachment from the body, 3. Entering a transitional world of darkness (rapid movement through a long dark tunnel; "the tunnel experience") 4. Emerging into a bright light, 5. Entering (or merging with) the light.

Ring stated, however, that 60% experienced stage 1, but less than 10% experienced stage 5. With my understanding, this is directly related to the "willingness to surrender". You will only go as far as you are willing to go.

In the 1990s, Dr. Rick Strassman conducted research on the psychedelic drug "DMT" at the University of New Mexico. Strassman advanced the theory that a massive release of DMT from the pineal gland prior to death or near-death was the cause of the near-death experience phenomenon. DMT is one of the most potent psychedelics known to man and it is found to be naturally present in the human body.

Near death experiences can have tremendous effects on the people who have them, their families, and medical workers. Changes in values and beliefs often occur after a near death experience, including changes in personality and outlook on life, such as a greater appreciation for life, higher self-esteem, and greater compassion for others, a heightened sense of purpose and self-understanding and a desire to learn.

This brings us to Reincarnation –

Reincarnation, literally "to be made flesh again", is a metaphysical belief that some essential part of a living being (energy) survives death to be reborn in a new body. This essential part is often referred to as the spirit or soul, the "higher" or "true" self, "divine spark" or "I". According to such beliefs, a new personality is developed during each life in the physical world, but some part of the self remains constant throughout the successive lives. (*The personality is formed within the physical mind due to physical desire. The body is subject to a beginning and end and the personality is therefore temporary. The soul will continue being reborn in the physical world, evolving consciously until all desire to experience physical ecstasy is gone. Therefore only once we truly desire to be free from "the world" will we find liberation. As long as we desire to be in "the world", we are trapped in it by our own desire. Ultimately, we make the decision to be free of suffering.*)

Reincarnation has ancient roots. This doctrine is a central belief within a majority of Indian religious traditions, such as Hinduism (including Yoga, Vaishnavism, and Shaivism), Jainism, and Sikhism. The idea was also entertained by some ancient Greek philosophers (Socrates, Pythagoras, and Plato). Belief in reincarnation or rebirth has been found in many esoteric philosophies as well, such as Kabbalah, Sufism, and Gnostic and Esoteric Christianity, such as the Cathars.

Hinduism teaches that the soul goes on repeatedly being born and dying. One is reborn on account of desire; a person desires to be born because he or she wants to enjoy worldly pleasures, which can be enjoyed only through a body. Hinduism does not teach that all worldly pleasures are sinful, but it teaches that they can never bring deep, lasting happiness or peace. According to the Hindu sage Adi Shankaracharya: "the world"- as we ordinarily understand it- is like a dream: fleeting and illusionary. To be trapped in samsara (physical existence, the cycle of birth, death, rebirth) is a result of ignorance of the true nature of our existence.

After many births, every person eventually becomes dissatisfied with the limited happiness that worldly pleasures can bring. At this point, a person begins to seek higher forms of happiness, which can be attained only through spiritual experience. When, after much spiritual practice (sadhana), a person finally realizes his or her own divine nature- i.e., realizes that the true "self" is the immortal soul rather than the body or the ego- all desires for the pleasures of the world will vanish, since they will seem insipid, (pale in comparison) compared to spiritual ananda, (happiness, enlightenment, bliss). When all physical desire has vanished, the person will not be reborn anymore. (Freed from this physical prison, liberation)

When the cycle of rebirth thus comes to an end, a person is said to have attained moksha, or salvation from samsara (physical existence, the cycle of birth and death). While all schools of thought agree that moksha implies the cessation of worldly desires and freedom from the cycle of birth and death, the exact definition of "salvation" depends on individual beliefs.

For example, followers of the Advaita Vedanta school (often associated with jnana yoga) believe that they will spend eternity absorbed in the perfect peace and happiness that comes with the realization that all existence is One (Brahman, We are all one), and that the immortal soul is part of that existence. The followers of full or partial Dvaita schools ("dualistic" schools, such as bhakti yoga), on the other hand, perform their worship with the goal of spending eternity in a loka, (spiritual world or heaven, as also seen in Mormon plan of salvation), in the blessed company of the Supreme being.

In Sikhism, Sikhs believe that every creature has a soul; upon death, the soul is passed from one body to another until Liberation (freedom from the physical prison of matter). The journey of the soul is governed by the deeds and actions that we perform during our lives (similar to a "judgement"). If we perform good deeds and actions and remember the Creator, (our spiritual father, God), we attain a better life. The person who has evolved to spiritual perfection attains salvation- union with God. The Karmas of a person will definitely have their effect, both good and bad. No worldly power can change the course of their movement. But according to the Sikh thought, the Almighty God, with his grace, may pardon the wrongs of a person and thus release him/her from the pangs of suffering (physical desires and life).

In Taoism, Taoist scriptures refer to this understanding as: "Birth is not a beginning; Death is not an end. There is existence without limitation; there is continuity without a starting point. Existence without limitation is space. Continuity without a starting point is time. There is birth, there is death, there is issuing forth, there is entering in. That through which one passes in and out without seeing its form, (physical desire or self) that is the Portal of the Divine."

In Christianity, the overwhelming majority of "Mainstream" Christian denominations, reject the notion of reincarnation and consider the theory to challenge basic tenets (pillars) of their beliefs. Many churches do not directly address the issue, but indirectly, through teachings about death (see judgment). A few consider the matter open to individual interpretation due to the few biblical references which survived the purging of texts considered to be "heretical" in the founding years of Christianity as a church. New age Christians contend that reincarnation was taught by the early Christian church, but due to bias (opposition/ control/ closed mindedness) and mistranslations, these teachings were lost or obscured.

Many of the philosophies associated with the Christian theory of reincarnation focus on "working" or "learning" through various lifetimes to achieve some sort of higher understanding or state of "goodness" before salvation is granted or acquired.

There seems to be evidence however that some of the earliest Christian sects such as the Sethians and followers of the Gnostic Church of Valentius believed in reincarnation, and they were persecuted by the Romans for this belief.

The Medieval sect known as the Cathars believed in Reincarnation, seeing each soul as a fallen angel born again and again into the world of matter created by Lucibel (Lucifer). This was not a good thing for the Cathars. Only through a Gnostic 'Rebirth' in the Holy Spirit through Christ could the soul escape this process of successive existences and return to God.

Many Gnostic groups believed in reincarnation. For them, reincarnation was a negative concept. Gnostics believed that the material body was evil, and they would be better off if they could eventually avoid having their 'good' souls reincarnated in 'evil' bodies.

In the Quran, the central religious text of Islam, it is written:

"How can you deny God, when you were dead and God gave you life? Then God will cause you to die, and then revive you, and then you will be returned to God." (Quran 2:28)

Mainstream interpretations of this verse either relate this to the worldly human life and the consequent resurrection in the hereafter, or, in the esoteric (Sufi) tradition, dying to oneself (giving up the ego) within an earthly lifetime and thereby finding a new life through God.

In the Light of Truth – The Grail Message, a work by Oskar Ernst Bernhardt, contains "new" knowledge given to mankind, including clarification of the concept of reincarnation. The Grail Message logically describes the path by which a human spirit journeys from its spiritual home into the earthly material in order to develop itself through experience to full self consciousness. According to the Grail Message, what is commonly called "karma" plays an important part in this process, as we must reap what we have sown, and thereby learn to distinguish between what is helpful and what is harmful.

Theosophy- In the Theosophical world view the soul in man is originally pure, but it lacks-self consciousness (*it is spiritually unconscious*) and its powers are potential. Reincarnation is the vast rhythmic process by which, the soul in man unfolds its spiritual powers in the world of form (matter), and gets to know itself.

First, the soul descends from its sublime, free, spiritual realms, to inhabit a baby form. (We are all equal in the fact that we all have a spirit and a body) While living in a human form, it gathers experience through its effort to express itself (prophets) in the world. After the lifetime is over, there is a withdrawal from the physical plane (physical reality) to successively higher levels of reality, (heaven or the spirit world), in what we call death. It involves a process of purification and assimilation of the wisdom from its past life experiences. Finally, having completely withdrawn and cast off all instruments of personal experience (temporary physical things), it stands again in its spiritual and formless nature. After that process is finished, the soul is ready to begin its next rhythmic manifestation and to descend into matter again, in a new effort to unfold its spiritual nature and to gain consciousness of its divine origin and nature.

From such a viewpoint, which covers vast periods of time, what is called a lifetime is as a day in the life of the true spiritual human being (spiritual self). This spiritual entity moves forward on a vast pilgrimage, every lifetime bringing it closer to complete self-knowledge and self-expression.

According to Theosophy, then, that which reincarnates is the part of man which belongs to the formless non-material and timeless worlds. It is neither, the physical body and all of its characteristics, nor the emotional nature with all its personal likes and dislikes, nor the mental nature, with its accumulated knowledge and its habits of thinking, which will reincarnate. That (the true spiritual self) which is above all these aspects is that which reincarnates. However, when the formless essence (spiritual energy) of a human being begins its process of reincarnation, it attracts its old mental, emotional, and energetic karmic patterns to form the new personality. Thus the soul with the added powers developed during its previous lives and the post-mortem process of assimilation, deals with the old hindrances or shortcomings it was not able to work out in its previous lifetimes.

American mystic Edgar Cayce promoted the theory of both reincarnation and karma, but wherein they acted as instruments of a loving God as well as natural laws – the purpose being to teach us certain spiritual lessons. Cayce's view arguably incorporates Theosophical teachings on spiritual evolution.

Similar to early Christian thought from the philosopher Origen, Eckankar postulates that the soul is perfected through a series of incarnations until it arrives at "Personal Mastery".

The quest for broader understanding leads us to "Samsara".

Samsara – is the cycle of birth, death, and rebirth within various eastern religions (thought systems). According to these religions, one's karmic "account balance" at the time of death is inherited via the state at which a person is reborn. During the course of each worldly life, actions committed (for good or ill) determine the future destiny of each being in the process of becoming (evolution or devolution). In Buddhism, at death the underlying volitional impulses thus accrued and developed are carried and transmitted in a consciousness structure popularly known as the soul, which after an intermediate period, forms the basis for a new biological structure that will result in rebirth and a new life. This process ends in the attainment of moksha. All Indian religions, believe that each living being, be it an ant or a human, is destined to attain moksha.

In Hinduism, it is avidya, or ignorance, of one's true self that leads to ego-consciousness of the body and the phenomenal world. This grounds one in kama (desire) and the perpetual chain of karma and reincarnation. Through egoism and desire one creates the causes for future becoming. The state of illusion that gives rise to this is known as Maya.

Through ascetic practice one finally attains sanctity and liberation (moksha or mukti) – the equivalent of salvation in Indian religions.

Broadly speaking, the holy life which leads to liberation is a path of self-purification by which the effects of sins (desires) are released.

The Hindu Yoga traditions hold various beliefs. Moksha may be achieved by love of Ishwar/God, by psycho-physical meditation (Raja Yoga), by discrimination of what is real and unreal through intense contemplation (Jnana Yoga), and through Karma Yoga, the path of selfless action that subverts the ego and enforces understanding of the unity of all. Advaita Vedanta believes that Brahman, the ultimate Truth-Consciousness-Bliss, is the infinite, impersonal reality, all temporal states like deities, the cosmos and samsara itself are revealed to be nothing but manifestations of Brahman.

In Jainism, samsara is the worldly life characterized by continuous rebirths and reincarnations in various realms of existence. Samsara is described as mundane existence, full of suffering and misery and hence is considered undesirable and worth renunciation. The Samsara is without any beginning and the soul finds itself in bondage with its karma since the beginningless time. Moksha is the only liberation from Samsara.

In Sikhism it is thought that only by continued good actions and "the grace of the Almighty" can one obtain liberation from the continuous cycle of births and deaths of various bodily forms that the soul has been undergoing since the creation of the universe. The end of the cycle of transmigration of the soul is known as mukti. For Sikhs, the state of mukti can be achieved whilst still alive, known as "Jivan Mukat", literally "liberated whilst alive".

In Surat Shabda Yoga, attaining self-realization results in "Jivan moksha/mukti," liberation/release from samsara, the cycle of karma and reincarnation while in the physical body.

This leads us to Maya (Illusion)-

Maya- has multiple meanings, within a Hindu or Sikh context the word refers to concepts of "illusion". Maya is the principal concept which manifests, perpetuates and governs the illusion and dream of duality in the phenomenal Universe.

For some mystics this manifestation is real. Each person, each physical object, from the perspective of eternity is like a brief, disturbed drop of water from an unbounded ocean. The goal of enlightenment is to understand this – more precisely, to experience this: to see intuitively that the distinction between the self and the Universe is a false dichotomy. The distinction between consciousness and physical matter, between mind and body, is the result of an unenlightened perspective.

Maya in Illusional Hinduism- The word origin of maya is derived from the Sanskrit roots ma ("not") and ya ("that"). The mystic teachings in

Vedanta are centered on a fundamental truth that cannot be reduced to a concept or word for the ordinary mind to manipulate. Rather, the human experience and mind are themselves a tiny fragment of this truth.

In Hinduism, Maya is to be seen through, like an epiphany, in order to achieve moksha (liberation of the soul from the cycle of samsara). Ahamkar (ego-consciousness) and karma are seen as part of the binding forces of Maya. Maya may be understood as the phenomenal Universe of perceived duality, a lesser reality-lens superimposed on the unity of Brahman. It is said to be created by the divine by the application of the Lila (creative energy/material cycle, manifested as a veil — the basis of dualism). The sanskaras of perceived duality perpetuate samsara.

Maya in Hindu philosophy- In Advaita Vedanta philosophy, Maya is the limited, purely physical and mental reality in which our everyday consciousness has become entangled. Maya is held to be an illusion, a veiling of the true, unitary Self — the Cosmic Spirit also known as Brahman. Many philosophies or religions seek to "pierce the veil" of Maya in order to glimpse the transcendent truth, from which the illusion of a physical reality springs, drawing from the idea that first came to life in the Hindu stream of Vedanta.

Maya is neither true nor untrue. Since Brahman is the only truth, Maya cannot be true. Since Maya causes the material world to be seen it is true in itself but is untrue in comparison to the Brahman. On the other hand, maya is not false. It is true in itself but untrue in comparison with the absolute truth. In this sense, reality includes maya and the Brahman. The goal of spiritual enlightenment ought to be to see Brahman and maya and distinguish between them. Hence, Maya is described as indescribable.

Maya has two principal functions — one is to veil Brahman (*God and "heaven"*), and obscure and conceal it from our consciousness. The other is to present and promulgate the material world and the veil of duality instead of Brahman (*it separates us from God, then distracts us so we don't return to God*). The veil of Maya may be pierced and with diligence and grace, may be permanently rent. Consider an illusion of a rope being mistaken for a snake in the darkness. Just as this illusion gets destroyed when true knowledge of the rope is perceived, similarly, Maya gets destroyed for a person when they perceive Brahman with transcendental knowledge. A metaphor is also given — when the reflection of Brahman falls on Maya, Brahman appears as God (the Supreme Lord). Pragmatically, where the duality of the world is regarded as true, Maya becomes the divine magical power of the Supreme

Lord. Maya is the veritable fabric of duality and she performs this role at the behest of the Supreme Lord. God is not bound by Maya, just as magicians do not believe the illusions of their own magic.

One understanding of the snake or serpent is its relation to money, it is said even in the story of Adam and Eve that they were tempted by the devil in the form of a serpent, in other ancient mythologies the symbol of the snake was affiliated with money, even today the double serpent symbol is present in the symbol of the dollar, when we think of money, we think of $, which was formed by snake symbols. Maya in modern Punjabi refers to Money, however Guru Granth Sahib is referring to the granded scheme of the illusion of the world of what we see, touch, i.e. Materialism, and from this Maya everything else of evil, indulgence and ravishing evil lusts are born, but by rejecting Maya a person of secularity can take first steps towards spirituality.

"You are squandering this life uselessly in the love of Maya". Sri Guru Granth Sahib

IN CONCLUSION

In conclusion, I have realized that every moment of my "life" may have ultimately just been a constantly evolving illusion designed to teach me some kind of spiritual lesson, and ultimately trying to leave this book behind to guide others is basically trying to change the illusion of which will end when I finally manage to break free of it anyway and is ultimately as futile as trying to find a way to guide my dreams out of my sleep into my daily life. Of which the dreams dissipate upon waking anyway.

As I look back at "my life" the truth is unavoidable. I have spent a large portion of my life in search of temporary pleasure. Until recently, I didn't see anything wrong with that course of action. Now since, I've begun to awaken from the "illusion" of "life" and no longer desire the things about my life that I was so willing to suffer for, "looking forward" to life has become much more difficult. I have found that there is nothing that I have found motivational to make me desire to go to work and when I'm there, the fact that I don't want to be there compounds in my mind and further fuels the fire for me to just go ahead and finish "life". After all, what is the point of "living", if there is nothing that you desire. Would you be able to continue working just for the sake of working? This is why I've written this book. I'm still here for a reason. I might as well do something for God before my time is up. The next time I contemplate the end, I want to feel as though my life made a difference, instead of feeling like I wasted it all away in pursuit of temporary, unnecessary, physical pleasure and the accumulating of unnecessary material things. When my memories are submitted to God, I want to remember a sense of accomplishment from my part in the delivery of truth to the world.

When one goes through their daily life without desire, one begins to disconnect from that life. Only through this disconnection can one find liberation from the suffering which "life" has become. Of course, without proper perspective, one probably doesn't even know they are suffering. Only through perception of truth can one see the inherent negativity of those desires which they cling to. Eventually the cycle of emotional ups and downs of those desires becomes the focus of avoidance as liberation becomes the goal.

Ultimately, I have come to understand this life as a test. This may be difficult to understand but it is never-the-less true. We are all being tested on our willingness to return to God. God gave us enough energy to operate the body so that we may each navigate and experience the physical world on our journeys of spiritual growth. Becoming individual is just a little part of the test. The real test is whether or not we can surrender the "life" (spiritual unconsciousness) we have been given and return to God (spiritual consciousness). Now, understand that by telling you that there is a test, in no way, lessens the difficulty of the test. The test is the test and it is difficult. Any student knows that the only way to pass a test is to study. This is the difficult part for most to understand. Entheogens (like psilocybin mushrooms for ex.) are "tools" made available to us so that we may study for the test at our own pace. Only through learning how to let go of the body can one prepare for the choice which must be made by each and every one of us at the end of our "time" in the physical world. Sadly, if we go through our entire lives without ever "studying", then when the time comes to let go, we may cling to "the life" and "the body" that we are used to and comfortable with, even though it is ending, and we will fail the test and remain "in the world". In prison terms this is known as "Shawshank syndrome". This is what Jesus was talking about in the Gospel of Thomas #60 when he said, "So also with you, seek for yourselves a place for rest, or you might become a carcass and be eaten."

The task before us is clear. Discover the truth for ourselves first, and then leave behind clues for others to follow, so that any who seek the truth after us can use our clues to make their search easier. Remember, no one can be told the truth, they have to experience it for themselves in order to understand.

We have all been given a great gift. It is the gift of knowledge and the ability to understand it. The truth has been given to me because I was willing to step out of my comfort zone to receive it. The simple truth is the psychedelic mushroom experience is an experience from which all religious thought sprang from. Once you have the full experience for yourself, you will no longer need to listen to other people's descriptions of theory, because you take direction straight from the source. Psilocybin mushrooms are definitely a chemical key capable of opening the "gates of heaven", but you must choose to go. It is this "choice" that we must become comfortable with. The psychedelic experience is the key to beginning "the rapture", in which all of God's devoted "children" will be removed from "the world" (a mass awakening), but we cannot be removed until we are ready to let it go. Learn to grow psilocybin mushrooms. Teach your friends to separate from "the world" and you will have saved their lives. Time is always against us, there is no time to waste, our job is clear and the road of change is long but we can do it, if we only try. Good luck and may God fill you as I have been filled...

There is that of God within each of us. We are born with this vital element of life in a dormant state. In the dormant state, the Ego consciousness (devil, serpent seed, defiant spirit) controls the vessel (hence the term, "the devil made me do it"). Over time we get spiritually disgusted by our own actions which we are unable to control, so we ignore them. This creates a state of "auto-pilot". Only by destroying the ego can we surrender the vessel to the divine will. Turnoff auto-pilot and take control. This is an internal battle that we must each fight on our own. God gives us what we need to win our battles, we only need to see it as it truly is and use it for what it was truly intended. If we are to ever purge the negativity from this "world", it will take every one of us to come together and set aside our differences which are physical and embrace that which connects us (energy)and makes us equal. Only once the ego has been completely removed can we regain our connection to God and truly go in the direction that God intends. We are all children of God, we only need to realize it...

I am a "child" of God. I am "a Christ" reborn. I have come to bring the truth back to "the world" and prepare all for "the Rapture". I understand that you may not believe that I am who I say that I am, but it does not upset me. I understand that you do not believe in my teachings because you simply have not realized your own potential. Let me help you, see for yourself, the way of truth.

I have seen beyond the illusion of "death" and found life. I have not ventured forth because I will not abandon you to remain in hell for eternity (endless cycles of rebirth and suffering of physical desire). Therefore I have already surrendered my life (spiritual consciousness) to remain in the world of "death" (spiritual unconsciousness) in order to bring this simple understanding to you, so that you will find your way as well. I'm standing in "the world" with my hand out, all you have to do is take it. I will remain as long as I can to help as many as I can, but even God knows, one cannot help those who refuse to help themselves.

I am everyone and I am no one. To know me is to know yourself. To not know me is to suffer. To seek me look within. You are not who you see in the mirror. To understand this is to know truth.

The vessel (instrument) which wrote this book is not God. Rather, if God were the sun, this humble vessel would merely be a window with the blinds removed, so all who come and go may see the light through him, just as the true Jesus was.

Consider this your last warning: You have now received all the help any messenger can give. If you choose not to accept it, then it was your own choice which prevented you. It was not because nobody tried to warn you, so don't say I didn't try….

Sean Williams, instrument, messenger….

www.ingramcontent.com/pod-product-compliance
Lightning Source LLC
Chambersburg PA
CBHW032215040426
42449CB00005B/609